SELECTED POEMS OF

Shmuel HaNagid

The Lockert Library of Poetry in Translation

Editorial Advisor: Richard Howard

FOR OTHER TITLES

IN THE LOCKERT LIBRARY,

SEE PAGE 235

SELECTED POEMS OF

Shmuel HaNagid

Translated from the Hebrew by

PETER COLE

PRINCETON UNIVERSITY PRESS

PRINCETON, NEW JERSEY

Published by Princeton University Press, 41 William Street,
Princeton, New Jersey 08540
In the United Kingdom: Princeton University Press,
Chichester, West Sussex

Library of Congress Cataloging-in-Publication Data

Samuel, ha-Nagid, 993-1056.
[Poems. English. Selections]
Selected poems of Shmuel HaNagid / translated from the Hebrew
by Peter Cole.
p.   cm. — (Lockert library of poetry in translation)
Includes bibliographical references.
ISBN 0-691-01121-4 (cl. : alk. paper).
ISBN 0-691-01120-6 (pbk. : alk. paper)
1. Samuel, ha-Nagid, 993-1056—Translations into English.
I. Cole, Peter, 1957– . II. Title. III. Series.
PJ5050.S3A23   1995
892.4'12—dc20   95-153

This book has been composed in Dante

Princeton University Press books are
printed on acid-free paper and meet the guidelines
for permanence and durability of the Committee
on Production Guidelines for Book Longevity
of the Council on Library Resources
Printed in the United States of America by Princeton Academic Press

3   5   7   9   10   8   6   4   2

The Lockert Library of Poetry in Translation is supported by
a bequest from Charles Lacy Lockert (1888–1974)

For Matt Cole

1958–1981

❊ CONTENTS ❊

FROM *Ben Mishle*: (After Proverbs)

FROM *Ben Kohelet*: (After Ecclesiastes)

✦ PREFACE ✦

THESE TRANSLATIONS were born in friendship and owe their existence to numerous people, including Adina Hoffman, Gabriel Levin, Harold Schimmel, Dennis Silk, Gidi Nevo, Aharon Shabtai, Ruth Nevo, Martin Guttman, Eli Gottlieb and Eliot Weinberger. I am especially grateful to Yosef Hayim Yerushalmi of Columbia University, for his curiosity and generous support of this work early on; to Matti Huss of The Hebrew University, who graciously answered my many hours' worth of questions; and to John Hollander, Marvin Hoffman, Rosellen Brown, Abdullah al-Udhari, and Eric Posner—who helped in various ways with the manuscript.

Along with all readers of medieval Hebrew poetry, I am also enormously in the debt of scholars who, over the last seventy-five years, have labored to rescue this literature from oblivion. There have been many, and more are emerging. In preparing these translations of Ha-Nagid I relied heavily on the work of David Solomon Sassoon, David Yellin, Jefim Schirmann, A. M. Habermann, Shraga Abramson, Dov Yarden, Dan Pagis, Yehuda Ratzhaby, Ezra Fleischer, Israel Levin, Gershon Cohen, Salo Baron, and S. D. Goitein. Without their extraordinary efforts it would hardly be possible for us to read HaNagid in the original, let alone in English.

Throughout this project I have also referred to translations of HaNagid by T. Carmi, Raymond Scheindlin, Leon Weinberger, David Goldstein and Hillel Halkin, and I have made extensive use of the ASV and JPS versions of the Old Testament.

Finally, acknowledgment is due to the National Endowment for the Arts, the Myrie Syrkin Foundation, the Gerbode Foundation, and Mishkenot Sha'ananim for their support of my work, and to the editors of the following magazines, where a number of these poems first appeared in earlier versions: *Agni Review, Conjunctions, Dark Ages, Grand Street, Poetry, Scripsi* (Australia), and *Sulfur.*

I

Medieval in the mind of the late twentieth-century thinker in the city acts a little like a quark: it conjures a trace, not an entity. If for certain readers the term prompts hazy recollection of monastic song, or death-by-plague, for others it means picture-book images of life on horseback under an eighty-pound suit of armor and a peculiar code of romantic attack. But for readers of Arabic and Hebrew poetry, *medieval* almost always leans against *Golden*—as in the Golden Age or renaissance of Moslem and Jewish culture in Spain, which took place some three centuries before Dante began sketching his Florentine colleagues in Hell, and was roughly contemporary in its first Arabic flowering with the Anglo-Saxon poet who sang, "For the doom-eager bindeth fast his blood-bedraggled heart in his breast."

Ezra Pound and several centuries of translators have set up something akin to an astronomer's arrangement of lenses and mirrors in which English readers can now see likenesses of nearly all the important poetry written on European soil from Homer on. The Hebrew poems of Moslem Spain, however, or Andalusia—what most scholars consider the greatest in postbiblical Hebrew literature—still hover in an occidental blindspot. This is so for a number of reasons, chief among them being that Andalusian Hebrew verse is grounded, aesthetically, in a culture westerners find only slightly more accessible than the Black Stone at its Meccan center.

Hebrew readers have had their blindspots as well, and these have naturally shifted with the shifting locale and attitude of the readership. For many centuries the secular Hebrew poetry of Spain had minimal impact on its potential audience which, owing in large part to circumstances beyond its control, was far more interested in explicitly religious material, or at most in the tradition of liturgical verse, or *piyyut*, whose frame of reference was restricted to the synagogue and its cycle of scriptural events. Only with the modern Hebrew revival of the nineteenth century and the reemergence of a strong, Enlightenment call to Jewish national identity did poets and critics return to the landscape of the medieval vision.

While an extraordinary amount of devotion, scholarship, eccentricity, and detective luck went into the retrieval of the neglected or actually lost secular poetry of the Spanish-Hebrew Golden Age, perhaps the most dynamic personality involved was that of Hayim Nahman Bialik (1873–

1934)—the leading poet of the modern Hebrew revival and a man who, like each of the major medieval Hebrew poets, in poetry and in life looked back to the biblical text for a route through to the future.

Particularly from his mid-thirties on, Bialik dedicated himself to the cultural process of *kinnus*, or ingathering: "From all the branches of our literature," he wrote, "from every corner in which a part of the 'holy spirit' of the nation is hidden ... we have to extract the best, scattered sparks, to join them together, to be united in the people's hand." This kabbalistically political call led Bialik to his activity as an essayist, publisher, editor of Hebrew legends and, prior to fleeing Bolshevik Russia and settling for a time in Berlin and then British Mandate Palestine, to "our Spanish poetry," whose situation he likened in 1923 to "a desolate plain of dry bones scattered with the stones and shards of a palace in ruins."

Bearing a charged relationship to his own concurrent silence as a poet, and working a kind of yogic permutation on his contemporary Osip Mandelstam's statement that "prose is addressed to a public, poetry to the providential addressee," Bialik joined forces with his old friend Y. H. Ravnitzky and set about preparing modern critical editions of two of the major Spanish-Hebrew poets, Solomon Ibn Gabirol (1021/22–c. 1058) and Moshe Ibn Ezra (1055-after 1135), planning to bring them out with Dvir, his publishing house in still sandy Tel Aviv. While abroad on a fund-raising trip for the firm in 1926, Bialik wrote Ravnitzky and his colleagues back at the office to report that he had come up with considerable financial support for their projects, but that word of the firm's books rarely made it to Berlin or New York or London. He berates his "dear friends" for their irresponsibility with regard to advertising and public relations, and tells them to get to work. This has gone on for five and a half printed pages in the *Collected Letters* when Bialik suddenly turns to literary matters and mentions—"to make you happy, Ravnitzky"—that he has with him a crate of old manuscripts, one of which contains Hebrew poems that had been lost for most of a millennium. "It is an incomparable treasure," he tells them,

> a discovery that will cause a sensation! Woe to our scholars, and woe unto us, that a pearl such as this has long been thrown about in the trash while no one saw fit to bring it out into the world. ... A kind of light shines on the marvelous prince—upon him and his period and the poets of his day. ... The man is unrivaled in our history. See for yourself and decide.

In hand was the diwan, or complete poetic works, of the eleventh-century Spanish-Hebrew poet and political leader Shmuel HaNagid. The manuscript had been passed on to Bialik by the scholar and bibliophile

David Solomon Sassoon, whose family collection of old Hebrew documents was among the most important in the world at the time. For his part, Sassoon laconically notes at the end of his preface to the first "complete" Hebrew edition of HaNagid's poems in 1934—they were published in London rather than Tel Aviv, after considerable delay—that he had purchased the diwan in Aram Tsoba (Aleppo). It is, he reports, a hard-to-decipher 1584 copy of an eleventh-century original, probably several times removed. He gives us the name of the copyist as Tam Ibn Yehiyya, then lists several of the manuscript's previous owners.

With Sassoon's discovery and the subsequent publication of annotated editions of HaNagid's poems between 1946 and 1963, what had been a scanty and generally obscure, minor body of poetry by an important Jewish personality was enlarged by a factor of eight, and Shmuel HaNagid was embraced as the first great poet of the Hebrew Golden Age—a poet whose synthesis of secular and religious longing in poetry could speak to post-Adolf Loosian readers as powerfully as it had spoken to the aristocratic audience of medieval Andalusia. Beyond that, however, and maybe of deeper interest to readers who, like E. M. Forster, picture the authors of all ages writing at the same time in a single reading room of a large library, is HaNagid's way of using biblical sources to collapse the present of his poetry into an eternal and messianically allusive past, while projecting out of that pastness and into its echo as present and present-to-come.

"In his days," wrote the thirteenth-century Spanish-Hebrew poet Yehuda al-Harizi, in a section of his rhymed prose, or *maqqama*, "there was the great Nagid, R. Shmuel HaLevi, of blessed memory, who, in the craft of poetry, bared an upraised arm, and brought the hidden forth to light."

2

If HaNagid were provençal—and many scholars have proposed the Arabic poetry of Spain, and by extension its Jewish cousin, as a missing link or premonition in the development of the Troubadour lyric (which Ezra Pound calls "a little Oriental in feeling")—his *vida* might read directly out of historian Abraham Ibn Daud's twelfth-century *Book of Tradition*:

> Besides being a great scholar and a highly cultured person, R. Samuel was highly versed in Arabic literature and style and was, indeed, competent to serve in the king's palace. Nevertheless, he maintained himself in very modest circumstances as a spice merchant. . . . Since his shop happened to

adjoin the courtyard of Ibn al-'Arif—who was the Katib of King Habbus B. Maksan, the Berber king of Granada—the Katib's maidservant would ask him to write letters for her master, the vizier Abu'l Qasim ibn al-'Arif. When the latter received the letters, he was astounded at the learning they reflected. Consequently, when, after a while, this vizier, Ibn al-'Arif, was given leave by his King Habbus to return to his home in Malaga, he inquired among the people of his household: "Who wrote the letters which I received from you?" They replied: "A certain Jew of the community of Cordoba, who lives next door to your courtyard, used to do the writing for us." The Katib thereupon ordered that R. Samuel be brought to him at once, and he said to him: "It does not become you to spend your time in a shop. Henceforth you are to stay at my side."

He thus became the scribe and counselor of the counselor to the king. Now the counsel which he gave was as if one consulted the oracle of God, and thanks to his counsel King Habbus achieved great success. . . .

Subsequently, when the Katib Ibn al-'Arif took ill and felt his death approaching, King Habbus paid him a visit and said to him: "What am I going to do? Who will counsel me in the wars which encompass me on every side?" He replied: "I never counseled you out of my own mind, but out of the mind of this Jew, my scribe. Look after him well, and let him be a father and a priest to you. Do whatever he says, and God will help you."

Accordingly, after the death of the Katib, King Habbus brought R. Samuel HaLevi to his palace and made him Katib and counselor. (Trans. Gershon Cohen)

Ibn Daud goes on to tell of HaNagid's work on behalf of Jewish communities from Sefarad, or Spain, to Babylonia, and this, for some eight centuries, was the legend of Samuel the Prince and gnomic poet. Though the fairy-tale aspects of Ibn Daud's account have now been exposed as heroic inflation (a suspiciously similar story is told about the Moslem chamberlain of Cordoba, Ibn Abi Amir, who also rose from retail obscurity to power through his pen), the gist of the preceding is accurate enough, and the historical record shows that Shmuel ben Yosef HaLevi, or Isma'il Ibn Nagrela—as Ibn Daud says he was known in the community—was born to a well-off Jewish family in 993 CE in the highly cosmopolitan and ethnically diverse city of Cordoba. He was given a classical education consisting of Hebrew, Arabic, and "Greek" subjects, including tutoring by the renowned Talmudist, R. Hanokh ben Moshe. It is also likely that as a young man HaNagid worked in the spice business, or large-scale international trade, the routes of which ran from the Sea of Darkness (the Atlantic) through the Great Sea (the Mediterranean) and across the Moslem empire to the Indus River and sometimes China.

When the Umayyad caliphate of Cordoba was overthrown by Berber forces in 1013, HaLevi fled south to Malaga and set up shop there. Within a few years he was appointed to the position of tax collector by the Berber court of Granada (essentially a position of community leadership—as it was easier to have a prominent Jew collect taxes from the Jews), but four years into his tenure he became involved in a dispute of some sort and was dismissed. Shortly thereafter he was chosen to be the vizier's assistant.

In 1027, at the age of 34, Shmuel HaLevi became the First Spanish Nagid, or governor of Spain's Jewish community. HaNagid (The Nagid), as he came to be known, continued to rise through the ranks of court officials, and in 1037 he was promoted by King Habbus's successor, his son Badis, to the powerful position of Chief Vizier of Granada and head of its Moslem army. He successfully led Badis's forces into battle for sixteen of the next eighteen years, serving either as field commander or in a more administrative and Pentagon-like capacity as minister of defense, or chief of staff. In his various public roles HaNagid helped establish Granada as one of the wealthiest and most powerful of the thirty-eight Taifa or Party States of Andalusia, and he continued to serve both Moslem and Jewish communities until he died, in 1056, reportedly of exhaustion after returning from yet another military campaign.

The preeminent cultural and religious figure of his time, he had earned, says Ibn Daud, "Four crowns: the crown of Torah, the crown of power, the crown of a Levite, . . . and the crown of a good name."

3

"His poems . . . are various and full of color, powerful in their contents, fine in their form, original in their ideas, and clear in their rhetoric," according to the Judaeo-Arabic of Moshe Ibn Ezra, the chief theoretician of the era. "All that pertains to his compositions and works and letters is known to the uttermost edges of east and west and across the land and sea, and up to the leaders of the Babylonian community and the sages of Syria and the scholars of Egypt and the Nagids of Ifriqiya and the lords of the West and the Spanish nobility."

Wherever one turns in HaNagid's verse, one finds the great antagonism between Arab and Jew woven into a peculiarly supple and at the same time metallic—possibly defensive—sort of beauty. Three books comprise the diwan: *Ben Tehillim* (After Psalms, or literally, Son of Psalms) is perhaps the most original of the three, as it introduces to post-biblical Hebrew poetry Arabic subject matter, a mastery of the new

Arabic quantitative meters, and an unforgettably personal cast to the essentially biblical language that the poets of HaNagid's time employed in an effort to purify their diction and outdo their Arabic and, by implication, Koranic models. This combination of subject, tone, and impulse aligns HaNagid with the martial/lyric spirit of Second Samuel and the Davidic Psalms, an affiliation HaNagid makes explicit at several points, once referring to himself as the "David of my age," and repeatedly invoking his Levitical ancestry.

In one psychologically bizarre and uncharacteristically long wine poem—some scholars classify it as a "boast poem"—HaNagid invites a number of the city dignitaries to his house for a party, where they drink themselves unconscious. When they wake at dawn and try to rise, "as though they no longer had toes, nor their backs the spines to prop them," they ask him, "Who *are* you and what *is* this?"—and he tells them:

> I am the heir of Kehat, the remnant of Merari,
>> men of renown, and excellent craft—
>>> and from my father to
>>>> Samuel, Elkanah's son,
>>>>> the blood lines cross.
> Likewise with Moses the prophet of God,
>
>>>> who is kin to me.
>> When the people are gathered I'll
> call him *my father*
>>> and he'll call me *my son*.
>> When the people are gathered.
> And they who question my lineage will find
>>>> their own much flawed.
>>> I have glory and wealth,
> though God alone knows strength and power;
>
> my songs surpass even those of the Levites,
>>> even those of the close-cropped priests...

The fourteen metrically identical hemistiches of the original (thirty-seven words in the inflected Hebrew and sixty in the English), placed near the end of the poem (the conventional position of the boast in the Arabic qasida), allude to or cite at least twelve biblical passages, using the mosaic-like ornament modern scholars call *shibbuts*, or inlay, as in the jeweler's art. The argument has also been made that the ornament more closely resembles the beaten gold and breastplate gems woven "with cunning work" into the priestly garment of Exodus 39.

Like so many Spanish-Hebrew conventions, the use of biblical phrasing was brought over from Arabic literature, where it was based on the Koran and was known as *iktibas*, literally, the lighting of one flame from another. Faceted or thread-like, derivative or, as some writers claimed, an opportunity for literary one-upmanship, the *shibbuts* was central to the Hebrew poetry of the period—including that of its most famous practitioner, Yehuda HaLevi (c. 1075–1141)—and poets employed it to such an extent that the verse frequently seems to become a web of quotation, with all the indirection, multiple meaning, and mirrored or magical effect that entails.

Sometimes the *shibbuts* borrows directly from the biblical usage, as above, and at other times it plants the biblical words or phrase in a totally foreign or contradictory setting, raising bristles on the back of the poem for the medieval audience, which knew much of Scripture by heart and would absorb the strangeness on impact. Most often, however, the biblical lexicon is used neutrally, as a kind of compositional raw material with which the poet as craftsman is free to construct even his most personal of poems, though that aspect of person is always inseparable from the poems' complication of nonvernacular tones. For the medieval Jew, wrote the twentieth-century theologian and translator Franz Rosenzweig, "quotation is not a decorative frill, but the very warp to the woof of what he has to say."

Just as much Islamic art thrusts all form to the front and sets up a vibrant arrangement of color and shape, then uses architecture to establish an underlying depth and sense of weightlessness, so the Hebrew poem in this context establishes equally brilliant aural tableaux, while relying on biblical echoes to create the illusion of time, or oddly lit ascent or descent through the past. The effect is similar to that described by the Arabic inscriptions on a fountain in the Alhambra's Court of the Lions— "Seeing this basin one thinks it ice, while the water melts from within it; but who can say, for certain, which of the two really flows . . ."—where the calligraphy helps to complete the construction in an experience that would be entirely different were the garden stripped of its *ornamentum*, or equipment (just as the poems would be essentially altered without their biblical element). This is perhaps what Jonathan Leverkühn has in mind in Mann's *Dr. Faustus* when, checking the modernist assumption, he says that "ornament and meaning always run alongside each other."

Working this elaborate weave of surfaces, HaNagid was able to fuse Hebrew and Arabic, given and personal, lyric and epic dimensions in what we now think of as his signature manner. Throughout the three books his poetry presents a compelling forward thrust and relative simplicity of diction, yoked by artifice to complexity of texture and thought.

HaNagid's second collection, *Ben Mishle* (After Proverbs) is technically less innovative than *Ben Tehillim* and focuses on dense, often piercing constructions that draw on the various traditions of the poet's acquaintance. It is likely these that Al-Harizi referred to when he said that most of HaNagid's poems "were hard and profound and would require commentary."

In what amounts to a personalized anthology of wisdom literature—including "adaptations" as well as "original" compositions—HaNagid often translates from Arabic models with considerable freedom and without acknowledgment. This was standard practice in HaNagid's time, and the often dominant and impersonal elements of quotation and convention did not prevent the audience from recognizing the authorial presence in the poem. More important than novelty was the activating touch of the poet in his ability to wed the available conventions with grace and memorable—some would say Byzantine—effect. In any event, the much-paraded medieval division of form and content makes little sense when the poem stands or falls on the quality of that touch, weighing out aspects of vision as though on the pans of a sensitive scale:

> He'll bring you trouble with talk like dreams,
>   invoking verse and song to cheat you;
> but dreams, my son, aren't what they seem:
>   not all the poet says is true.

HaNagid develops a similar consideration of opposites in what Ibn Ezra refers to as the most mature and sublime of his compositions, *Ben Kohelet* (After Ecclesiastes), a book that consists of epigrammatic verse, descriptions of natural phenomena, and mortality poems of various lengths. Like its biblical antecedent, the collection comes off sounding uncannily familiar and modern in many of its concerns. Technically *Ben Kohelet* contains some of HaNagid's most brilliant work, including "Gazing Through the Night," "At One or Two the Child," and the aural tour de force, "The Market," whose Hebrew builds its nightmare of vanity by repeating the single rhyme of *dahm* (blood), as the poet's eye takes in the slaughter:

> Avarti al shuk tabachim / bo tsoan u'shevareem alyadahm,
> U'miree'im rav k'degat hayam / v'oaf la'roav ba yom aidahm,
> Bo dahm kapha al gav dahm, bo/shochtim rabim yareeku dahm. . .

Before the virtuosity of the above and its continuation—later in the poem we get to the line

> lo nimtzah et lo met bo met / o et lo yoleed moleedahm

—the translation swerves like Stevens's bucks, "because of the firecat," i.e., further from the Hebrew than usual, hoping to get what it can.

4

> *"And if you plan to bring a matter from Arabic into Hebrew,*
> *grasp the spirit and intention of the work, but do not transpose*
> *it word for word, for not all languages are alike."*
> —Moshe Ibn Ezra, *The Book of Remembrance and Discussion*

Throughout these translations of HaNagid's poems, I have tried to account for my understanding of the poet's distinctive combination of pathos and wit, his integration of artifice and the steady pressure of the personal in his lines. As HaNagid and his school developed a hybrid poetry of native and borrowed elements, one that blends rigorous formal constraints with a big-blocked biblical vocabulary drawn from an essentially free verse, so I have ranged in my seeking English equivalents for his Hebrew effects. For example, I make no attempt to duplicate the quantitative meters of the poetry—an inherently problematic task in English—but have chosen instead to retain one of the effects of that meter, an approach to rhythm and sound that highlights the physical quality of the movement from syllable to syllable, yet preserves the weave and rhythmic impulse of the poem as a whole. By the same token I generally soft-pedal the end rhyme of the Hebrew, which repeats a single syllable throughout the poem (for up to 149 lines), something the uninflected English resists, except in the shorter proverbs. Instead, I work with a more contemporary sense of internal and off-rhyme, assonance and consonance, mirroring the Hebrew where I can, and breaking the original hemistiches down for parallel or transplanted effect when I cannot.

In other words, I nudge the internal frame of the poetry off center, hoping to echo its original presence without forcing the English into elaborately awkward compromise—though here it is also important to admit the need for an undertone of archaism in the work, and the considerable problems posed by the use of "unrevealed" translations of a sacred and now largely unfamiliar text in a poetry that relies so heavily on scriptural quotation.

Technical and theoretical considerations notwithstanding, my aim has been simple: I have translated to conduct the poet's quality of emotion and movement of mind. When the voice in the Hebrew is ambitious or subtle or aggrieved, or where the verse is particularly musical, inventive, or sublime, I try for a similar sense of the English. The courtier rabbi-poets of the Spanish-Hebrew literary renaissance were not the prissy egg-shell steppers that most translators and many scholars make them out to be. They were, as Gershon Cohen makes clear in his commentary on Ibn Daud, men of great learning, fierce ambition, and complex talent and spirit. They were pious, but in a manner that translates poorly into our own assumptions of faith.

In approaching this work I have also tried to keep in mind that many of the innovations of the new Hebrew poets of Spain represented a radical and controversial break with the insular synagogue poetry that had been practiced throughout the Jewish world since the fourth century, and that the Eastern *piyyut* was violet to the distant red of the Arabic qasida on which most of these innovations were based; that, when the Jewish poets of Andalusia began turning to their Moslem counterparts for new poetic models, they were seeking to extend the range of motion in their minds, to revitalize the weave of their language, to equip themselves for their world.

If in the twentieth-century West new forms of artistic expression have meant, to a large extent, forms commensurate with the effect of technology and automation, and involved mining the past for models that would help overthrow the stale conventions of a previous era, in eleventh-century Andalusia it meant forms that would allow Arabic-speaking Hebrew poets to react to the sophisticated world of Moslem Spain and the expanded and sometimes confusing role that Jews were playing there. That their particular break with the literary past involved, at one and the same time, a return to classical diction, a challenge to conservative social and ideological lines of thought, an advance to intricate structures and new, "imported" subject matter, and the adoption of a fundamentally ornamental poetic is a move that eludes many contemporary readers, for whom poetic form is all too often reduced to its reactionary or knee-jerk-experimental impulse, and only in rare and happy instances employed as an imaginative device. Cheerleaders, Blue Angels, the guards at Buckingham Palace, and a carrot are equally formal, as are Merce Cunningham's dances, and those of mating sparrows. The relevant question is not whether a work or its translation is formal, but what kind of form it employs and where its emphases of pattern will be; what effect its ornament, or lack of ornament, conveys; how well a given convention or norm has been established—in or beyond the work—from which one might depart; and what the relation is between that (imminent) departure and (potential) return.

Poetic content, like food, never gains in separation from form; and levels of diction as well as percussive and tonal arrangement determine tension and effect at all points in the poem, not merely at the end of a line, or metronomically along it—just as the shifting colors of rooftops, clouds, and sky in a day (let alone the words we use to describe them) literally widen one's eyes and change the shape of one's face. The man who wrote "I am the heir of Kehat," "The Market" or

> . . . the friends who fray me,
> their fine physiques and
> slender thinking,
> thinking it's ease or gain
> that drives me,
> pitching from place to place,
> my hair wild, my eyes
> charcoaled with night—
> and not a one speaks wisely,
> their souls blunted, or blurred,
> goat-footed thinkers . . .

with full awareness of the Arabic and biblical conventions on which he built his verse, that man had more in mind than diversion, linguistic macrame, or the entertainment of perfumed companions sipping through life in the capital. Military, political, and religious accomplishments aside, he was an exceedingly ambitious artist with an abiding if complicated love for the Jewish past and an obvious passion for his cosmopolitan present. For all his efforts to establish what has been called a neo-Solomonic kingdom in Andalusia, he was a man very much of his time and cultural arena.

Readers of a conventional stripe who have Hebrew will perhaps question these attempts to portray that man, or one like him, in not-always-metrical English that faces backward but knows it is nearing the year 2000, and they may be inclined to call these adaptations. All translation adapts or comments, as Ibn Ezra suggests it should, all the more so translation of a poetry that, like medieval Hebrew, requires annotation even for contemporary Hebrew speakers. Given its numerous obstacles the very notion of translation from medieval Hebrew requires an imaginative leap or sleight of hand. In making my way over to a credible English, I have tried nevertheless to be as literal as possible in action. Readers who want to reconstruct that action, in painfully slow slow-motion, would do well to turn to the originals (and notes) in the editions of Dov Yarden, A. M. Habermann, and Shraga Abramson. Those who have no Hebrew but find themselves within reach of an English Bible or two—preferably the King James and the 1917 Jewish Publication Society version—would gain from reading several of the translated poems and their notes alongside the Scripture to see how the *shibbuts* and the other medieval Hebrew ornaments function, for there is little like their combination in English, except perhaps glancing aspects of the English court poets and the School of Donne in places (though the diversity of individual poetries, along with the differences of moral style between Christian England and Judeo-Moslem Spain, neutralize for me all but the most schematic of resemblances).

Whatever one calls these poems, they are the work of translation in the sense that the Hebrew and, I believe, all poetry is: namely, they aim for the translation of a sustaining poetic reality, not just an attractive or surprising series of words. It was this reality that first drew me to HaNagid twelve years ago when I began reading his remarkable chain of elegies for his brother Isaac, this that Bialik wrote of in the 1920s when he called for the "ingathering of our Spanish poetry," and this that I have sought in the following, and its like throughout the diwan:

> The multiple troubles of man,
>   my brother, like slander and pain,
> amaze you? Consider the heart
>   which holds them all
> in strangeness, and doesn't break.

• • •

To translate, according to the dictionaries, is to "bring into the afterworld without causing death." That, in a poetic nutshell, is what I have aimed for—though not without sacrifice, and not without loss.

Jerusalem
January 1993

❖ AN ANDALUSIAN CHRONOLOGY: ❖

The Background

711–756 CE

Combined Berber and Arab army of some 7,000–12,000 troops crosses the Mediterranean at its narrowest point and lands at the tip of the Iberian peninsula, then part of the failing Visigothic kingdom. The great majority of this force consists of Berbers newly converted to Islam, though there is also an Arab minority. Led by Tariq ibn Ziyad, the invasion is carried out under the aegis of the Islamic caliphate and the Arab commander, Musa ibn Nusayr. (The rocky promontory Tariq lands near now bears his name in fossil-like fashion: Gibraltar—a collapsed form of Djabal al-Tarik, the Hill of Tarik.) Through diplomacy, warfare, and, it seems, the help of a sympathetic Jewish community that had suffered under Visigothic rule, the Moslem army conquers most of the peninsula within seven years. The new Moslem frontier is in flux for the next forty-five years, during which time the area has twenty-two different governors.

The name Andalusia, as Moslem Spain came to be known, seems to derive from Vandalicia, which is what the Vandals called the peninsula they crossed in the fifth century (CE) on their way south into Africa. The term al-Andalus first appears on coins as the translation of the Latin name, Spania.

750 Several years of civil war in Syria and Iraq result in the overthrow of the Umayyad caliphate of Damascus, which had established a Moslem empire from the Atlantic to India. The new dynasty is that of the Abbasids, who move the center of power east to Iraq. Baghdad is founded several years later (762 CE) and a Golden Age of Arabic culture begins to take shape. The arts, sciences, and learning flourish in this cosmopolitan court culture, and poetry in particular emerges from the desert landscapes of the pre-Islamic odes (qasidas) and becomes to a much greater extent the expression of urban individuals. Subject matter is diverse, formulation sharp, and artistry complex. This Golden Age of Arabic literature lasts for some five hundred years, and has a profound effect on both Jewish and Moslem cultures in al-Andalus.

756–929

The last surviving member of the Damascene Umayyad dynasty flees to al-Andalus and establishes himself as Emir Abd al-Rahman I in Cordoba. He brings together a diverse population of Berbers, Jews, native Andalusians, and Slavs—northern Europeans who were brought into Andalusia as mercenaries and slaves. Abd al-Rahman I proves himself a strong ruler and is able to establish diplomatic ties with North Africa, the Byzantine Empire, and Christian kingdoms to the north. He also maintains cultural links with Abbasid Baghdad and emulates earlier Umayyad achievements. Perhaps the most prominent civic project of his reign is the construction of the Great Mosque of Cordoba, work that is continued by his successors for the next century and a half. As a poem of his written at the estate he called al-Rusafa indicates, Abd al-Rahman I was driven by the sense of longing that so many Arabs, Jews, and other culturally displaced people in the region would eventually feel:

> In the midst of Rusafa a palm
> has appeared in a Western land,
> far from the home of palms.
> So I said: This is me—
> for I, too, am in exile,
> far from my family and friends.
> In exile you have grown tall,
> and alike we're far from home.

In 928 Egyptian-born Sa'adia ben Joseph (882–942) is appointed to the Gaonate of Sura, Babylonia, the most influential position in the Jewish world at the time. Sa'adia Gaon, as he comes to be known, translates the Bible into Arabic, redacts the first standard prayer book, writes an important work of Jewish theology, develops a rhyming dictionary, and writes commentary on the Bible. His *Book of Beliefs and Opinions* is the first systematic attempt to present Judaism as a rational body of beliefs; it includes modern-sounding chapters on money, children, eroticism, addiction to eating and drinking, and the satisfaction of the thirst for revenge.

929–1031

Sa'adia's "scientific" spirit makes its way west into al-Andalus in the person of his student, Dunash ben Labrat. Dunash (d. 990) introduces Arabic poetry's secular genres and quantitative meters to Hebrew, and uses the Arabic meters in liturgical Hebrew verse. He is accused of "destroying the Holy Tongue."

Dunash and the other Hebrew literati of his day are members of the Cordoban court of Hasdai Ibn Shaprut (c. 915–c. 970), the first great patron of Jewish letters in Andalusia. Also a prominent physician and statesman, Ibn Shaprut serves the Moslem regime as customs minister and de facto minister of foreign affairs to Abd al-Rahman III. He holds important meetings with delegations from Byzantium and the Holy Roman Empire, and negotiates peace treaties with the kingdoms of Leon and Navarre to the North. As the Nasi, or leader of the Jewish community, he establishes ties with the Jews of Italy, Provence, and the Khazar kingdom of southern Russia.

Ibn Shaprut's support of the early Andalusian Hebrew poets Menachem ben Saruk and Dunash ben Labrat is crucial to the development of Hebrew letters in al-Andalus, as is his appointment of the refugee Moshe b. Hanokh to the rabbinical seat of Cordoba. The appointment of b. Hanokh is perhaps the central factor in the loosening of ties between the Jews of Andalusia and the great center of Jewish cultural life in Babylonia. Hasdai supports Jewish scholarship and recruits teachers from the centers of Jewish study in Palestine and Babylonia. Under his leadership, Spanish Jewry becomes independent and learning thrives.

Abd al-Rahman III assumes the title of caliph in 929, and his successors develop Cordoba into a city to rival the Abbasid capital of Baghdad. This is a golden period for Hispano-Umayyad art and culture. Cordoba becomes famous for its exquisite silk fabrics and leatherworks, and exports from the region include slaves, paper, expensive and durable garments, and new agricultural products developed with advanced irrigation and farming techniques adapted from the East. The textile industry of Andalusia is so integral to the region's economy that one important scholar has described it as the Andalusian equivalent of our stock market, or our steel industry at its height. Thousands of men are employed in the construction of the royal city of Madinat al-Zahra, near Cordoba, which has accommodations for scholars, a small army, and a harem of 6,300. From the East and often up through North Africa, immigrants stream into this new Moslem metropolis, musicians and poets prominent among them, and—mutual suspicion and internecine warfare notwithstanding—for a brief period of some 150 years, Berbers, Slavs, Jews, Arabs, and native Christians coexist economically and culturally in what Spanish historians call Convivencia.

Abd al-Rahman III's son, al-Hakam II, makes important additions to the Great Mosque of Cordoba, which comes to symbolize Moslem power and accomplishment in Andalusia. The Capital is renowned for its urban sophistication and revolution in manners, its arts and sciences, and its libraries, which far outdo those of the Christian west.

Shmuel ben Yosef HaLevi (Isma'il ibn Nagrela, as he is known in Arabic literature) is born in 993 to a prominent family in Cordoba. When civil war breaks out in 1010–1013, Ibn Nagrela is among the many who flee the city. He eventually settles in Granada, where he quickly rises to power in both the Jewish and Moslem sectors, becoming Nagid, or governor of Andalusian Jewry in 1027. The title is most likely bestowed on him by the Babylonian leader, Hai Gaon (939–1038), though it is possible he is self-appointed. (From hereon in he is referred to as Shmuel HaNagid.)

1031–1086

In 1031 the Caliphate finally falls, and numerous city-states (Taifa) mod-elled on the dispersed court of Cordoba are established throughout al-Andalus. HaNagid leads the powerful state of Granada in its rivalry with Seville. He also establishes a highly sophisticated Jewish court, sponsor-ing belles lettres, religious study, and the production of books, and he corresponds with Jewish communities throughout the Near East and Maghreb. HaNagid dies in 1056 and is succeeded by his son Yehosef. In 1066 Yehosef HaNagid is assassinated during a popular uprising and many Jews are massacred in Granada. The Taifa period comes to an end some twenty years later with the invasion of the Almoravids, a Berber regime that had risen to power in North Africa and crossed into Al-Andalus.

From *Ben Tehillim*: (After Psalms)

❴ YEHOSEF'S PREFACE ❵

Said Yehosef, the son of our Teacher, Shmuel HaLevi,
may God protect him: I have gathered in this book what
has come to me from the metrical work of my father and
teacher, may the Lord lift him in honor, and I wrote these out in
my own hand when I was eight and a half years old, it being that
my birth, according to my father's precise records, may God
sustain him for me, took place at three hours and four fifths of
an hour and two-thirds fifth of an hour exactly, on the night of
the third day of the week, before dawn on the 11th of Tishrei,
4796 according to the reckoning of the world [1035 CE], and
before dawn on the 11th of Dhu-alkaada, 426 after the Hejira.
I began this collection near Passover 4804 [1044 CE]. What
I gathered in this diwan was taken from his longer metrical
works and from the shorter rhymed poems that were sung before him in various meters. And though some speak of desire, he
wrote in full faith, referring to the congregation of Israel and its
God, as in the manner of several of the prophetic books, and God
will reward him in his intention. One who would cast aspersions
on this allegorical work by suggesting any other aim will
bear the burden of his guilt. . . . I ask for help from
the Lord, since all is in His hand.

ON FLEEING HIS CITY

And this in his youth on leaving Cordoba:

Spirit splits in its asking,

and soul in its wanting is balked;

and the body, fattened, is vital
    and full—

    its precious being uneasy . . .   5

But the modest man
    walks on the earth with his
    thought drawn toward sky.

What good is the pulse of man's flesh
      and its favors   10
    when the mind is in pain?

And the friends who fray me,
    their fine physiques
    and slender thinking,
    thinking it's ease or gain
      that drives me,
    pitching from place to place,
    my hair wild, my eyes
      charcoaled with night—
and not a one speaks wisely,   20
their souls blunted, or blurred,
    goat-footed thinkers.

Should someone unguilty
         hold back from
longing toward heights like the moon?   25
    Should he wait,
    weaving its light across him
like a man stretching taut his tent skin,

until he acts and they hear of his action,
30   as he adds and then adds like the sea
        to his fame?

By God and God's faithful—
    and I keep my oaths—
I'll climb cliffs
35 and descend to the innermost pit,
    and sew the edge of desert to desert,
      and split the sea
        and every gorge,
    and sail in mountainous ascent,

40 until the word "forever" makes sense to me,

and my enemies fear me,
    and my friends in that fear
      find solace;

then free men will turn
45   their faces toward mine,
      as I face theirs,

and soul will save us,
    as it trips our obstructors.

The beds of our friendship are rich with it,
50   planted by the river of affection,
      and fixed like a seal in wax,
        like graven gold
in the windowed dome of the temple.

May YAH be with you as you love,
55   and your soul which He loves be delivered,

    and the God of sentence
      send aegis,

    beyond both the sun and the moon.

THE MIRACLE AT SEA

And he sailed the sea in his youth with merchants and they
encountered a beast called tinyya *by those who know the creatures*
of the sea, and they have established that no one who met this creature
at sea has ever escaped in peace, and after a great struggle, God
saved them from its wickedness, and he recited this poem in
which he described what happened:

Is there poise for the stumbling and fallen,
    or rest for the wandering and lost?
And for me when I slip, or my fault when I fail,
    is there offering?

By the lives of all who'd come   5
    to console and assist the stricken
        by the life of each who came
    when I was in need and saw me panicked,

could it be there's never respite from anguish,
    that desolate land is desolate forever?   10
        But God restores what He levels,
though He keeps His secrets and erases His ways.

Listen to a word and know that not for lightness
    does the Lord sustain us on earth,
and take your reversals with an open heart,   15
        silence, and guarded thought.

Harden your ears to the brokers of spirit
    and turn your eyes from its whores,
      from Hophni at Shilo, or Zimri and the woman
from Midyan, or Onan—and his brother's widow.   20

Listen to a word and exalt the Lord
in the house and street, when you rise and lie down;
      shudder for dread and anxiousness.
    Worry, and let awe infuse you

25 for the God of beginnings unborn and unbearing,
         of lasting life without likeness.
      Return to His grace,
and face Him forever through fear and rebuke.

I am the man who went down to the sea
30   which most of the year is loud.
      It was August. I chose to go
         when the waves don't break in anger;

and we worked the oars and a wind came up
         as over a field of corn,
35 and the sea, like a slave, did as I asked,
         like a maid, and the sky was sapphire—

and the water like butter or virgin oil.
And the sailors told of all that they'd seen
         of wonder on board,
40   and one spoke of a marvelous creature,

and another called it a beast—
      and the captain answered:
None of you know of the miracle sea—
         you haven't fathomed a thing.

45 There exists a monster whose name is Karchah,
         singular among the abysmal shapes,
      it devours all who feed on each other
         and kills the survivors with fright.

It overturns ships, and fleets with their crews,
50 in its mouth they're flipped like a chariot.
         He hadn't finished his story
when lowing and raging the creature appeared.

I heard it: thunder or the sound of a throng
         seemed still alongside it;
55 and I looked at its terrible form,
         wrought like a fish or book-like Leviathan,

the torturous serpent like a palm tree in stature,
         its head huge as a galley with oars,
      its face haughty, like a hill,
60   its eyes like pools,

---

its spout like a furnace, its brow like a wall,
　　its mouth wide and deep as a cave;
quenching its thirst it would empty a river
with its lips like swollen wineskin on wineskin,

and between them the hole　　　　　　　　　　　65
　　as though in a coat of mail.
Its flank was white, its back—green,
its neck like a tower, its belly—a mound,

　　its fin like a polished sword,
and its scales like a shield made red;　　　　　　70
its girth to us seemed like a cliff in the heart
　　of the sea. And it circled the ship,

　　though the fin was still,
and swam alongside it and rose on its tail,
　　like a cedar or climbing vine.　　　　　　　75
And everyone's heart melted like wax,

or like water, and the whirlpool engulfed us.
　　Then I calmed and steadied my soul,
as the lamb on the day of her slaughter goes dumb,
　　and called on my Lord,　　　　　　　　　　80

as others beside me called on their own,
　　like Ashemah . . . And I said:
In truth, and one way or another,
transgression takes the guilty soul;

if Jonah was swallowed up by the sea　　　　　85
　　and vomited onto dry land
　　in his righteousness—what of me?
My Lord, let me live, who wakes from his sleep.

If this is reward for the work of my hands,
　　may my sin be absolved . . .　　　　　　　90
Then it sank in the dark of the sea,
like a soldier that God had thrown in its parting;

　　but under the ship it threatened,
as our hearts died, our breath failing.
　　And the Lord rebuked the being,　　　　　95
for the moment returned to its depth—

———————

the little worms
saved on a pitch-covered bough.
He raised the dead from Sheol
100   and saved the swallowed with a hand held high.

The nautical wizards were astonished,
and wondered how it could happen—
with their ships trapped by Karchah, the accursed!
And I told them:

105   Such is deliverance for those who know
the great glory of the Lord in His fullness.
He sends salvation to those who admit Him,
and vengeance to those who provoke His wrath.

The sea is His, and all its creatures,
110   and the waters below, which are vast;
He hangs them on nothingness.
What is a beast beside the Rock

who shaped it and granted it breath,
then endowed it with power?
115   I thank the Lord with a song of redemption
my mouth will remember,

and acknowledge the Rock beyond creation,
without completion,
and grant the truth of resurrection—
120   that the dead will arise from dust;

that the Book of Moses we have in our hands
is true and composed with perfection;
that the words of the sages are worthy
and their study is sweet—

125   and reward for the righteous will follow,
as the dead for their sins in secret
receive their recompense;
that the Lord rules—over land and sea

and the sky and Great Bear above;
130   that His fear in the lines of my face is drawn,
as His Law is drawn through my blood.

A CURSE

And a poem in which he describes his wandering:

Intrigue taunts my
    heart like a pennant

on a ship's mast, in a storm;

and exile is ink
    in God's book

across my soul, and every shore;

  and all on whom wandering is
    written are

driven like Jonah, and scavenge like Cain.

THE APPLE

*And he mentioned being at his house where one of the poets recited a
poem about a bowl of fine and beautiful apples which were brought
before him. One of the company translated the poem into Hebrew.
And then they implored him to respond with a version of his
own, and he improvised the following:*

1.
I, when you notice,
    am cast in gold:
the bite of the ignorant
    frightens me.

2.
An apple filled with spices:
    silver coated with gold.
And others that grow in the orchard,
    beside it, bright as rubies.

I asked it: Why aren't you like those?
    soft, with your skin exposed?
And it answered in silence: Because
    boors and fools have jaws.

3.
The grape was created for gladness,
    to banish our grief;
and virgin oil— for pleasure,
    and the apple— to sniff.

4.
Those apples in a bowl
resemble the high priest's jewels;
    so keep them far away from
    the hands and teeth of fools.

5.
Why does the loudmouth in company,
    whose tongue never ceases to wag,
break no teeth on biting the apple
    and downing the gold not gag?

6.
The covenant of brothers at court while drinking is dual: 25
    One: Pull out the tooth that would bite the apple;
        Two: banish the fool.

JASMINE

Look at the jasmine, whose branches are green
    as topaz, and its stems and leaves—
while its blossoms are white as bdellium.
    With carnelian red in its shoots
it looks like a pallid boy who's shedding
    the blood of innocent men with his hand.

THE GAZELLE

I'd give everything I own for that gazelle
who, rising at night to his
harp and flute,
saw a cup in my hand
and said:
"Drink your grape blood against my lips!"
And the moon was cut like a D,
on a dark robe, written in gold.

THE FAWN

I'd give everything I own for that fawn
who betrayed me—
my love for him locked in my heart.
He said to the rising moon:
"You see how I shine
and dare to be seen?"
And the circle was set in the sky
like a pearl in a dark girl's palm.

WHERE'S THAT COY GAZELLE

Where's that coy gazelle,
  and the scented fawn
    with his calamus and myrrh?
As the moonlight cancels the stars,
  my friend, rising
    canceled the moon.
He sang to me softly and leaned
  on the giver of song to swifts
    and doves in their season.
He tried to say *no* but said *slow,*
  and I did as his tongue required.
    He wanted *wrong* but said *thorn,*
and I rushed to the hedge of those roses.

IN FACT I LOVE THAT FAWN

"In fact I love that fawn,
    cutting roses in your garden—
which is why I've earned your wrath.
      If you could see him,
    the others would never find you."

"Scrape me some honey
    from your hive," he said.
"I'll have mine from your tongue,"
I replied. Then he bristled
    and said to me, sullen:

"And sin before the living God?"
"The sin's on me," I answered, "my lord."

I'LL SHOW YOU A FAWN

I'll show you a fawn who'll wound
   your heart with his eyes,
just as you're wounding mine with yours.
He's a blessing who made your heart
     cold as snow when I called you,
   and sent up flames for you inside me;
He who sends strength in you and your weapons
     over the men of arms and war—
where a few are slain with a thousand arrows
while you, with one, slay a thousand more.

THEY STOLE MY SLEEP

They stole my sleep—now I'll steal theirs—
and shoot at them as they shot at me.
They won't find rest, as the woman said:
"Not mine, not thine; divide it."

HIS BROTHER'S ILLNESS

And my uncle Isaac fell ill, God have mercy upon him,
in the year 4801 [1041], and his heart went out
to him and he said:

My limbs thicken with
      strong premonition,
   and my vision
blurs with tears as it sharpens;
   and grief is budding   5
      along my mind,
   like weeds after
rains that smother the furrows.

Pleasure recedes
      and sickens me now.   10
  What good is sweetness
when one's brother lies ill?
    Let me make account
and not, my Lord, him, for my weakness.
     If I err —   15
would you punish another?

Then what of the error,
   remaining within?

ON THE DEATH OF ISAAC,
HIS BROTHER

And his brother's illness worsened and he decided to set out toward him
with the doctor Abu Madin and [. . . .] to him with news of his death
on the way and this was Thursday the 25th of Iyyar, 4801
[1041] and he composed the following:

I rushed to my brother who was,
    they told me,
      now weak in his illness and failing,
when a messenger approached and was still.

5   "Is Isaac alive?"

        "Already dead," he answered.

        Then I cursed him:

"Be deaf and have dust in your mouth,
and learn in your life each instant of sorrow:
10   May your parents mourn you.

      Haven't I called for a doctor?
And hasn't he healed many others like Isaac?

How could such wealth of spirit falter?
Prized by his peers, a gift to his people—
15   he sleeps."

And he said to me,
"Can one who took ill and then died awaken—
      whether poor or in power?"

        • • •

   First
child of my mother,
    death's
angel your specter,

soon the sun
setting will turn you,
   and by evening
      stones divide us—
earth's dust your shroud.   5

Neither splendor nor   10
   wealth could help you
      in your affliction,
   neither capital nor cup.
     I kissed you—
your heart wouldn't have it,   15
though you lay like a healthy
      man asleep.
   I wept,
but you wouldn't reply,
your tongue held   20
   from speaking.

And you slept
the sleep of forever
     the Rock
   topples   25
    and pours
across His design.

They'd given you wine
  in the cup of
    ancient death   30

  I'll drink from soon.

        • • •

Why should I force
  what custom requires
when my heart feels
like a moth-eaten shirt?
And why mourn in the   5
  dirt beside him,
when thinking reminds me
  of slime-filled pits?

23

Grief has broken my
    body's bearing;
why should I shatter
pitchers and cups?

The torn clothing
    will long be sewn,
when my heart still stings
as though ripped with thorns;
    and the walls of my strength
        will weaken with pain,
    after my clothes have been
        beaten and washed;

and sorrow will cling
    to my leaning frame,
like staves
in the rings of the ark.
But rest and happiness
    beyond my brother

will hover forever
    strange to my mood.

• • •

My language,
    I'd ask of you
in my life
to lift up a sound
    of lament
    for my brother and father,
who was father to all who were broken
in judgment,
    and the widows deceived;

who was generous and opened his doors
    to the street,
    when others were locked,
who'd herd as one the heifer and bear,
    and none devour,
        and none make prey.

I bathed him and dressed him
  and placed him in bed,
    and into my
  mouth came the voice of labor,

and I brought him to his grave,   20
my clothing torn,
    my family gathered,
  and I rose and went down

and helped him
  toward the world below.   25

They said:
  "He has taken him up."

  And I thought:
"Let Him take me instead."

And they said: "Time will   30
  heal your hurt and you'll rest."

And I answered in pain:

"On your balm of time
  and all rest beyond
    my brother—a curse!   35

Take, My Strength, my soul—
for grief such as this it can't carry."

                    • • •

And I returned,
  my spirit anguished.
    God be gracious
to you my brother,
buried the day   5
  before yesterday,
and now my mind is bitter.

Peace to you,
  who maybe hears me
  calling with all my power.   10

———————————

25

Answer me: Can you find
my voice through the weeping?
And how have you slept
in your tomb of dust below?

Have your bones let go?
Do your teeth show through?
Has your life-blood fled
in a night
as tears fled falling from me?

Firstborn of our father,
I've left you
with Him who drew me,
and on my word
you'll move
toward peace through my promise.

. . .

Tell him, please,
whom I long to see—
my hands released him
to Lostness:
By the life of the Living
God, for the world
he'll be in my blood
like fire,
until I'm dust
in the dust at his side.

. . .

Could condolence persuade me?
Is there solace, or hope in his wake?
And what is knowledge beyond my brother,
or life after leading him down to his grave?
Please don't stare, and save your speeches.
Thank you for coming;
stand over there, opposite,
yes, further off.

Recommend me now to the jackal who mourns—
he'll befriend me;

then tell him to wail while I'll wail—
    and see whose hauntedness carries.

But don't, friends, liken my suffering to Suffering,
or this breach by Isaac's death to your breaks.

• • •

Give up, heart,
    on bringing him back—
        on ever again
    seeing his likeness:

pledge yourself now to abjectness,   5
    and then, whenever you ask for
        strength in your grief—
            to dying his death.

• • •

When the name Isaac is called out across me,
    and my soul splits and my bitterness shows,
and others confront me, upright as I fail—
        their mouths full of laughter,
        their voices a song to my fall—   5

    and I act the horizon
like Joseph, as they gather about me—
how could I weep when they take such
        pride in seeing me crushed? My brother,
        with my own hands hidden in sorrow—   10

as though I'd never loved him like soul
    as a child, not shared a room,
        and the way to school—
whom I drew down to the pit with my will:
Death's shadow and dirt have replaced me,   15

as though you'd never been for me strength
        and a refuge in pain.
Quicken my being borne to the dust;
keep me from looking upon my wretchedness.
    I think of you now in bed as I rest,   20

and the memories steal
    sleep from my eyes.
As I eat I recall you fasting in darkness—
and the meal in my stomach is venom within me.
25   And I think of you thirsty,

    in the grave, as I drink,
and my tears unsweeten my water and wine.
    Light of my eyes, which dim,
      and my wound, which widens,
30   was it you alone we left that day of my ruin?

What of the others?
    My brother, did you long
    for the missing family around you
and draw to you ghost-like spirit to warm you?
35   Their dying won't help—and measures my own.

Now I despise the lids of my eyes
    and forever will loathe my slumber:
what was done to your corpse will be done soon to mine.
    From the first news of your parting,
40   I've feared for my failings:

let your death be reproof both to fools and the wise.

• • •

A brother is in me
    whose letters
  were like water
when my heart was thirsty.

5   Now, when others' come,
    not his,
the thought of him writing
    within me is fire.

• • •

Twelve months have passed—
    and you still haven't fled
      the fowler's snare.

Are the clods of earth so sweet to you now
that to us you prefer worms and decay?   5
    You were the best of us:
  Come back to your place with the elders,
and we'll talk of my battles and latest campaigns.

  Though how could he rise—
      whose flesh is rotting,   10
          whose bones are like dry trees?
  Imprisoned in earth, as his soul is in sky,
as the moth-maggots eat through his leathery shroud,
      and into his skin, like leaves.

                    • • •

Time, which betrays us,
why do I long for my brother, and thirst?
What does it mean? If you've stolen him
    from me— will he return?
      How? And when?   5
My eyes with his death have dimmed;
does it please you to see me now
      blindness's friend?

For you, Isaac—long in the grave
      and not to return,   10
    I weep and lean.
I bought with your death
    heart's knowledge, and craft,
  which during your life confused me:
I thought for my sake you'd live forever,   15
      but time meant other.

                    • • •

A psalm to the hearer

of prayer in my spirit forever.
  To praise Him is proper
      who metes out justice   5
      to the children of men,
like the sun for all revealed in its sky.
All who govern hard in their power,

---

first He created youthful and soft,
10 like grass and like labor,
like everything born,
and the poplar and oak.
But grief He created strong in its birth,
and weak in its growth,
15 and wherever it festers
in a thinking heart—
heart is lost.
From God-without-name to people is grace
neither language nor speech can measure.

20 I'd said in my mourning despair
would quickly wear through my heart
which, with worry,
like an alley had narrowed,
but now with solace is wide—
25 and my sorrow sheds
like the flesh of my brother.
If my heart is stirred and at times I weep,
and the sadness still rises within me like hosts—
more often than not I'm calm like a man
30 whose heart is empty,
his burden light.

So the Rock wounds
and then heals the stricken.
May He who blankets the sky with night,
35 and wraps my mother's eldest with dust,
forgive my brother his errors—
and in His grace remember his goodness—
and with our fathers
who were pure and His treasure,
40 count him as treasure.

THE FRIENDS

*And this in which he describes friends and people who spread a rumor
to the effect that the stars had decreed a brief life for him and
rejoiced at the prospect:*

My heart is a walled
           city inside me,
where I guard the love of my friends—
though I wouldn't compare my companions,
let alone the circle of friends of their friends—   5
    among them some like a hand beside me,
and others more like superfluous toes.
They greet me with warm regards and concern;
    they curse me behind closed doors.

But I have an eye that will not sleep   10
    and a heart whose net is spread
        over their secrets and sees
    into their innermost thoughts.
They teach me, whose way is just, and say:
    He who keeps your trust,   15
    place his trust within your heart
      and guard it well.
      Endow it with love—

like a daughter born among sons:
    grant it your care.   20
But he whose respect is heartless:
    tenfold return his scorn.
You'd fool with me—though you're the fools,
    and slander me,
        whose soul is rare.   25
    You mock me to strangers behind my back,
then treat me in person with awe and respect.

You take delight in the sorcerer's saying
    the stars predict that my death is near,

30   and hope for the fruit their evil will bear.
        Though how could the barren hope or give birth?
            The secret is God's,
                    He's hidden it from me,
            in wonder, withheld in His thought;
35   and if I'm brought to my end in strength—
        and death is the fate of all the living—

            in every city you'll hear:
        come and mourn—for a man who excelled in his age,
            before both the learned and Law.

THE HOUSE OF PRAYER

And this about men he came upon and heard studying their Talmud in
a sloppy manner, and he described them and their teacher:

Could time turn on its scholars?
  Or have they turned on the Law—
and bequeathed it to stuffed old fools in robes
  and every boor who declares:
    "I'm Mephibosheth,"   5
or "Hai the renowned is like Tsiba my servant"?
One needs, it seems, only fringes, a turban, and beard
  to head the Academy now. My brother,
    remember the day we passed
the House of Prayer, the Day of Willows,   10
  and heard up close a donkey bray
    and cows cry and low? And I asked:
  "Is the Lord's House now a dairy?
    This is a sin and disgrace."
And they told me: There are no fatlings or mules   15
  in the House of the Lord; they're studying Talmud.
    Then I answered from Scripture:
  "They've changed the instruction and Law;
    and as for me—wither?"
So we walked on, in anger, into the House of my God—   20
you couldn't help find it—and saw the teacher and students
    bobbing their heads like fronds,
  as their mouths abused the names of the great.

  And the teacher expounded at length,
    preying on every sound they made,   25
and I sat there enraged at the sight,
  and my soul grew sad . . .
  I asked the good teacher after his health,
    but he answered as a man of strife—
  and he started reciting the hundred blessings   30

in a coarse voice, like an army or horde,
and he thanked the Lord
who had made him a man and not a woman.
And I told him: You flaunt your phallic soul,
but the Lord will prove you hollow.

THE CRITIQUE

In which he responds to someone who sent him a weak poem:

I'd pictured your poem like the king's daughter,
    a man's delight, a woman of pleasure;
or a burning fire set by the hearth—
    in its corners calamus, cassia, and myrrh.

And I found it exquisitely copied—   5
    all the vowels were precisely arrayed.
In the past, I'd seen poems by your friends,
    but they were obscure, while yours amazed.

Your discourse flowed like the purest water
    for ablution— but this new one's a stain.   10
You've been for me like a precious son,
    whose standards I'm obliged to maintain.

So, hone your poems and their subjects,
    and know that each in its way moves toward
a day of judgment. And fear the critics,   15
    whose tongues are polished and sharpened like swords.

THE PAIN

In which he complains of a dull man who clings to him:

Your depth knows no bounds;
    you're an angel of God, not a man.
Your name reaches up to the stars
    and needs neither ladder nor wing.

I'm imprisoned by someone beside me
    whose climbing knows no end.
He has no sword, but he slays me;
    he plagues me without murrain.

What can I do with this Sisera?
    You're the only Yael I've got.
Come quickly and be like Abram
    with Chedorlaomer, captor of Lot.

WHAT ARE THESE

And this about the fireplace burning before him during the winter
with the figures of birds all around it:

What are these
soulless birds
given to flames
of light forever?

They'll never fly
in the warmth
of light   to distances,
and won't

by light be eaten.

A DAY OF DISTRESS

A day of distress and anguish,
   and I think of your message.
     You're fair,
and justice shapes your mouth and heart.
5 I remember your words which calmed me
     when trouble came near,
   and hope for your view and deliverance.

In all of your goodness you'd sent your servant—
   in bed, still a boy—
10   seraphs to greet me.
   They sat alongside me, and Micha'el spoke:
Thus saith the Lord, who contends in your cause:
When you pass through the waters I will stay you,
   and the rivers will not overwhelm you

15   *when your enemies come.*
   And Gabriel, too, his companion
     beside your chariot,
       heard of my fate and reported:
When you wade through fire you will not be burned;
20 *I will speak to the flame which will not harm you.*
   These are words I've held like a sword.

Though I stand before swords, I count on your blade.

THE VICTORY OVER SEVILLE

*And the rout of Ben Abbad's men took place toward dusk on the same
day [October 4, 1039] and Ben Abbad was killed early Friday night
on the eve of the Festival of Booths [October 5, 1039] and he
[HaNagid] recited this poem, and called it a Song of Praise:*

For me will you fashion acts each year
    as you have for the sages and fathers,
      and offer up lions like sheep,
    and slaughter their young as goats?
Every year will I pass through the sea   5
    as it opens a path before me;
every year will I walk through fire
    as you turn its flames to dew?

To you, my Rock, praise is fit,
    you are Lord, your hand is power;   10
those in retreat you entice at the end,
    with vengeance you take up the dross.
In the gates I will tell of your glory,
    and give thanks to your name in the people's midst;
I'll speak of your wonders where the righteous gather,   15
    of your marvels to those who wear fringes.

You redeemed me and ransomed the wicked
    on a day of misfortune this time last year,
      but after the death of Ben Abbas,
    Ben Abbad's approach gripped me with fear.   20
    The two had pursued me—a crown on one,
      and the other of lesser renown;
the former lifts kings to their kingdoms,
    and it's he who brings them down;

nobles are set with his seal over lands,   25
    and then deposed as he pleases;
to him the Berber princes attend—
    the Arab viziers praise him:
awaiting his charge as the year's first shower,

---

30 they hope for his word as for rain.
  Between him and my king there was envy,
    and each remained in his land.

  Both were sons of cedar-like kings,
    and others beside them were saplings;
35 both had long since preyed on kings
    and leveled their heroes with swords.
  Rulers and masses they'd slain as one;
  they slaughtered the mighty as rams;
    and no one could stop them in Spain—
40   there were none to resist or rebel.

  So he set out seeking a war,
    and stood with his men at the border.
  On his way he had taken a city and kingdom,
  and none in the land could put him to shame.
45   Lords to his troops were like slaves,
  and the healthy fell ill with their fear;
    his army's leaders were legion,
    and banners flew over his men.

  An insidious people now dwelled in his land,
50   who'd scorned the children of God
    and stoned them with words of abuse.
  They plotted against them, seizing their arms,
    and setting their legs in shackles,
    searching out mothers in Israel,
55   destroying both high and low—
  infants suckling along with the weaned.

  When their king's heart grew haughty,
    he spoke and we thought that he mocked us.
  So we set out toward his land with our columns,
60   seeking revenge for the kingdom he'd taken.
    Lion-like warriors were with us,
  and soldiers like locusts in swarms:
  men weighed down, though not with flesh,
    not from the fat on their loins.

65 All in their wrath who'd bear armor,
    all who'd strip their robes in war,
  and all who'd hasten toward the sword,
    all who'd run toward death with joy;

with coats of metal mesh like waves
    and shields reddened as parchment, 70
on horses like clouds rushing and flying,
   with rounded helmets and greaves;

their hands not full of lances and spears,
    like tamarisk trees—
the flashing of swords alone could be seen— 75
   no more was heard than their shouts of joy!
And after the burning and rout we withdrew,
    our arms loaded with spoils.
But his spies approached him with words
like silver's dross, or watered-down wine. 80

They plied him with reckless lies,
   as though they conspired against him;
and the Lord confused their reports,
   as though the advisers were children.
And as we retreated they urged him: 85
   Why sit in the fortified city
and not pursue the crushed?
   Why not plunder the weary,

or hurry to cut off the stragglers?
   So he rushed to depart in pursuit as advised 90
with his hundreds and thousands of men,
   and they stood before the Rock at the river,
    stood prepared for the fight—
and raised a triumphant sound like pipes.
His men and their arms were superior 95
   to those of the fallen Agag:

those we'd faced in the eyes of their foes
   had been women, while these were men.
   When they rode they raced like asses,
    and on foot like hinds or gazelles; 100
their dress was of royal design and adorned,
   and each on his head wore a crown.
In their might, their hosts, and their power,
   the parable makers were richly endowed.

When I saw their armies— 105
   unlike the Amalekites slain and despised—
when I saw the children of might afraid,

---

while heroes and warriors trembled,
and officers bowed their heads toward battle,
110   while leaders drew back from the fight;
I remembered the way that they'd slandered my people,
and how they'd weakened and crushed them

while the wicked divided their plunder,
casting lots for their lands;
115   when I saw the angel of death in my eyes,
and men in the battle dying before me,
I raised the name of the Lord,
gloried and feared in the heavens.
I'd set it deep in my heart,
120   to implore the dweller on high in distress,

to overcome forces with faith in His force
which gathers up men by the handful!
For me the fathers entreat the Lord
at times like this with a cry and petition—
125   and from the dust with cords of prayer
salvation is drawn and taken.
In their righteous perfection they advocate justice
and manage to turn back His wrath.

Mine is the Lord who told me: Trust
130   and I'll see you're content with your path;
for you I'll break the young lions' teeth,
I'll bring down giants before you!
Then He dressed himself in anger,
like the day when Pharaoh's men were drowned;
135   and He was revealed before us—
though not through a window in secret,

not from behind a lattice or wall.
He routed his foes, who fled like chaff
driven out from the floor of threshing;
140   He watched as they withered like leaves.
He made them afraid—
and they skipped like calves,
like kids or like wild young oxen;
and He stripped away their might

145   and left them in battle like children.
As angels diverted their sword thrusts,

confusing their right hands and left,
   others subverted their plans,
and made of his strategists fools;
lies He placed in the mouths of his spies,   150
on the lips of the enemy princes,
    to put them to death like churls—

and as soon as they saw what they chased,
   they fled in seven directions.
Surely this is the work of the Lord   155
   who tempted them into action,
who tangled their arms in ropes,
   and smothered their hearts with lids,
as their chariots blocked their retreat,
   and their horses hemmed them in!   160

With the breath of His mouth He cut them down,
like strands in the hands of a weaver, like thread,
   and I saw as their nobles were captured,
    and in fetters led to the king.
Some were left alive by his word,   165
   and others at his signal were slain;
and I wearied of watching the beatings,
   the stricken sinking in blood,

as soles that hadn't yet felt the earth
    were threshed with thorns;   170
and the wounded fighters were killed,
   and the corpses discarded like beasts.
On the eve of the sixth we chased them like quail,
    like a swarm of bees we pursued;
we struck down lords and kings,   175
   their slaves and princes alike.

They lay on the ground like dung,
   their heads like dung in the dust;
together swept from their cells,
   from their spacious chambers and halls,   180
and we seized those who would seize us,
and feasted on those who would make us their meal.
   They'd thought us already their chattel,
   but they were bequeathed in our cause;

185   they'd trusted their swords and spears,
      while we were saved by the Lord
whose name is great among gods.
And all who'd shackled the people
      were shamed and placed in bonds;
190   and they saw the terrible wonder in action
      which renders the evil their due:
      with His wrath He toppled each giant,

like a fetus expelled from its womb;
He dealt with the rich like worms in His fury,
195   with the bravest soldiers like ants.
      I saw you roar like a lion,
as you crushed the lions and roared,
      dispersing their hordes you cried aloud;
you were there and my enemies groaned
200   through their gut like a moaning lute;

you raged and kings were helpless
      to endure your anger and wrath.
Without having seen us they rushed to fight,
      but lagged when we came into view;
205   their bows were useful as straw,
      their worthless arrows were gravel.
The judgment was set on the second,
      and the sentence came down on the fifth;

and you reached in your servant's trial
210   through Arab and Berber alike,
and shadows grew long as you saved the sons
      of Might—in its month—from pagans.
So the year came to a close,
      as salvation flourished like a crop,
215   and you were my place of hiding in war,
      you delivered me from the unclean.

You stretched out your hand to save me,
      and brought my foes to pain,
and destruction's angels dispersed,
220   shaking the earth and sky.
Weapons of fury they sent like rain,
      and wrath they sent like showers;

and I drank from the cup of salvation,
    and the enemy drank the poison you served;

and you brightened the eve of the Harvest Feast,   225
    brought light to my darkened paths,
like the night of Abram and Moses' night,
        like Joshua's day with the sun.
I've strictly observed the times of the Lord,
    observed them like the dwellers in tents—   230
the Sabbath and Day of the Horn and Atonement—
    the Feast of Pilgrims and Booths.

And the fear of desecration was in me
    like fire, as others went slack:
the Lord established the days of rest   235
and my soldiers were all held back.
So I sing a doubled song to the Lord
    for the double miracle He wrought:
He scorned those who scorned us,
    and gave to the modest at heart;   240

I'll sing His praises and tell the people
    in exile and time to come,
even if all the children of earth
    and sky disdain to praise Him!
While the people brought to the Feast of Booths   245
the mountain myrtle and branches of palms,
    the Rock in His palm raised me:
        His booth hid me like a fort.

As they brought their willow He set the plains
    for His servant like a bulwarked city,   250
and He gathered my enemy's glory,
    while the citron was gathered from trees;
and the thick branches atoned for my soul,
    like a burnt offering or coins.
He was magnified over the water,   255
    by the watered willow and palm.

As my foes approached to consume me,
    I rose and they fell in grief;
and my heart hurt—but the Lord
    sent ministering angels to heal me.   260

He commanded them and they helped me,
  in descent from on high and ascent;
while over the people who'd sought my people
  for spoils—they parceled out pain.

265 We'll build our booths in gladness,
  while they still mourn in shame,
and delighted we'll chant His praises,
  while they in grief respond.
Is this for me—more worm than man,
270 despised among the humbled?
What am I or my life my Lord—
  but endless transgression and trouble!

I'm small and unripe for salvation
  and all the mercy you've shown,
275 and if in the world my merit's rewarded,
  if I'm repaid in accord with my acts,
how can I stand in the day of judgment—
  how would you pardon my sin?
To the strong Lord, revealed in the storm,
280 in the whirlwind over the pagans,

who will not lend His glory to others,
  nor bequeath to idols His praise,
I've already sung a song of triumph,
  and now a psalm of light like stars—
285 replete with a suitable number of lines,
  as befits a psalm of praise,
whose matter is worth more than pearls,
  whose lines with pearls are strung.

The mother of song is barren,
290 unable to bear one like it,
and song's fathers are likewise bereft.
As long as I live I'll keep them
as bracelets around my wrists—
  as rings run through my ears.
295 May they make my case when I'm judged
  with words dripping aloe and myrrh.

Recite, my people, this psalm beside me,
  and set it above all songs of praise;

46

establish its words as is right and in order,
   in the mouths of the elders and young!   300
And when in the future your children ask:
   "What *is* this?"—the asked should say:
   This is a psalm of praise
to the Lord who redeemed His friend,

who composed it for the redeemed: 305
   a psalm of praise, of greatness and glory,
to the Lord of Glory and His works which are great.

THE DREAM

And the the kingdom's governor, Abu Jaffar ibn Abi Musa, was aided by Ben Abbas in his plot [against HaNagid], but things went well for him after the death of Ben Abbas and one night while he slept he saw [in his dream] that he was reading the following verses:

Already Ben Abbas and all of his friends
and kind are lost:
Praise to the Lord be renewed!
And the ruler with whom he'd had counsel
will swiftly be beaten like fennel—
and crushed.
Then what of their grumbling,
their filth and all their control?

Hallowed—hallowed be the Name of my Lord.

THE WAR WITH YADIR

*And Yadir the commander came to the place known as Argona in the
year 4801 [1041], and with him were Wasil and Muwafaq, both of them
well-known officers among the Andalusian leaders, and they overcame
Argona and killed the commander of the city. Afterward they marched
to a place known as Samantin and overcame most of the castles there.
And then our forces went out against them and the hand of God was
with them and they killed Wasil and Muwafaq. And Yadir fled until
he was trapped at Cordoba and he was taken from there and
imprisoned in the castle of Munekar. And my lord my father
spoke of what happened to him and how he fared, praising
God for having granted him this great victory:*

Look away from me friend—
   open your heart, and hear my plan.
Would you scare me with false accusations?
What would I fear— with the Rock as my light
and salvation? You've been in my circle,   5
but if you persist in your slander,
   I'll count you as alien and cruel.
No good could come of one
   who exalts himself over my family,
no peace to him who threatens my city.   10
If you can't keep from your mouth's evil,
and insist on rebellion, like the House of the Rebel—
turn to me, friends, and listen,
     then weigh his word against mine.

He disputes my alliance with kings.   15
   This, I say, is my lot and inheritance.
He fears the face of their wrath.
   My refuge and hope, I respond, is in God.
What are these battles to you? he asks.
   And I answer: The place of my death   20
and burial is set, and the Lord who sent me
   seraphs in a dream will save me.

If I were rotting away with sin could I stop it?
   My book holds my destiny!
25   There are people who die before their time,
    like Zimri who reigned for a week, or Tivni—
      and others who face neither struggle nor war
but are buried just like the Egyptian, whom Moses saw;

there are those who are swept away
30   for want of righteousness,
    and others in life who go hungry, poor and alone.
Leave off me now—maybe I'd spend my days in prosperity,
    a turban above me; I'd drink still water
from my well in the cup of deliverance—
35   and running water drawn from my river.
      Is it right to despise my inheritance,
    and not rejoice in my portion and fate?
If your heart hurts for my future,
    and refuses to fathom my wealth and splendor
40   because of the fire and water I come through year by year,
    fear, my lord, for your own as for mine,
    though you're healthy at home, and calm.

I trust in the Lord who humbled my foes
    in snares concealed for my footsteps
45   when the enemy came to the garrisoned city
    and slaughtered its vizier like a calf.
He was a foe in the line of my king—
and the evil of strangers pales
    beside the evil of kin.
50   Two of the Spanish princes were there,
    and the Zemarite troops, and they seized the city
then advanced like a pestilence, destroying the fortress.
    We went out to stop them,
      and He broke them before us,
55   and August discovered their heads on stone,
    not in the orchards and grass.

We brought them down to the ground
    like birds of the air who had raised
      their wings on high;
60   we chased them in clusters of four and five,
    like olives from a tree the worker has beaten.
    We slew them two against three,

---

like long vowels against short in a word;
we struck them the blow that had leveled
      the armies of Og and Sihon. 65
The princes were stricken, reward for their obstinence,
      and all of it ended,
   except for the nine who fled—Yadir a tenth,
   pursued until he was brought like a gift,
      or tribute, that summer to my king. 70

My friend, for me in my straits
   the Rock rose up,
therefore I offer these praises,
   my poem to the Lord:
He recognized fear of Yadir in my heart 75
   and erased it.
      So my song is sung to the healer:
   He ravaged my enemies with pain,
      easing my own.
   Someone objected: 80
   Who are *you* to pay homage?
I am, I answered, the David of my age!
He responded: Is Saul, too, with the prophets?
      And I told him:

The heir of Merari, Sitri, and Assir, 85
   Elkanah, Mishael, Elzaphan, and Assaf!
How could the poem
   in the mouth be improper
      to the God who heals my wound?
   From Jeduthun the singer of psalms 90
   my father descends,
      and I from my father.
For the Lord I sweeten my song in its discourse,
   as He embitters my enemy's heart.
As He has pledged to vanquish my foes, 95
   so I've pledged my song to soothe him—
   to worship him day by day in my labor,
      as daily He pays my wage.

ON LIFTING THE SIEGE

*When those who were laying siege to Lorca heard that the troops were
approaching the city, they quickly fled, and our army sped toward
Lorca and camped there, where he wrote me the following:*

Send this pigeon, a messenger,
  although she can't speak,
    with a brief letter tied to her wings,
  dipped in saffron and scented with myrrh.

5   And once she's off and away,
    send on another. If one falls prey
  to a falcon or net's mesh, or delay—
    the other will cover, hurrying on.

When she reaches the house of Joseph,
10   she'll thrum from the rafters,
        flutter down to his fingers,
      and humor him, like a sparrow;

he'll loosen the knot at the note
and read: Know, my son, as you hold this,
15   the cursed enemy has fled
    and scatters itself on paths and hills—

like chaff driven by wind,
    or shepherdless sheep confused—
  without having seen its enemy except in surmise.
20   On our way to the rout they fled into darkness,

bringing death on themselves and each other—
        in panic crossing the river.
  They who had hoped were humbled,
      at a walled city held fast,

like a thief caught in the storehouse;   25
the look of disgrace like a cape to their faces;
         the shame to them clinging
    like the caul that covers the liver.

And they drank from the beaker of scandal,
         drank deep and were drunk!   30
I'd had in my heart the fear of death.
    like that of a woman's first labor—

but the Lord came across it,
         like a downpour in drought,
and my eyes brightened, as my foe's went dim.   35
    For gladness itself I sing,

         while he moans dirges.
Now my home is the voice of delight,
    his of bilious complaint.
To you, my Rock, my highest tower,   40

my soul sings out:
    in my need you had mercy prepared.
Put your heart, my son, in the hand of my God
    and bring these praises before the people.

    Make them an amulet bound to your arm—   45
to be cut on your heart with a stylus of iron and lead.

YOUR MANUSCRIPT SHINES

And he had me copy in my youth and promised me compensation
for every notebook, and I sent him what I'd copied and then
he wrote me the following:

Your manuscript shines
    like inlays of emerald,
its margins arranged
    like a robe well-embroidered,
        a feast for the eyes
          like a tree's first figs,
its scent like myrrh on the perfumed bride.

Read and inscribe
and focus your heart on the Law of the ark
              and its curtain—
    as you add,
    I'll add to your fee: Yehosef,
write with an iron pen in your book,

and be written within me,
        and not on my skin.
    Love for you
to the walls of my heart
        and its chambers is held:
my rebukes have been open, my love concealed.

TO YEHOSEF, HIS SON

*And I was sick with algudari, which is boils, in Tammuz 4804 [June
1044], and he was camped at Estiga and they hid my
illness from him until my condition had improved and then
wrote him about it. And he wrote me these stanzas:*

Heart's grief like sharp arrows—
   through me as never before,
though we'd met no resistance;
      then why this sorrow?
I thought of Yehosef, my faithful,
   in my heart a continual wound,   5
      for hearts understand
what comes to their love across distance.

For eight days he suffered
within me. How do we manage,   10
      or carry despair, our flesh
         not made of brass,
our strength not that of stones?
   On the ninth day they told me
      Yehosef is ill,   15
covered with boils and weak from fighting,

his bones full of fire,
   his mouth full of sores.
He'd been stricken with pain
      for eight days—   20
   graver than eighty of evil.
And the heads of all who came to visit
were fountains of tears, their eyes like pools,
though they said that his fever had broken,

      the pain receded,   25
and the white boils burst on his skin;
that his eyes were shielded by the Lord's
      hand, which shields all

55

who shield their faith. Yehosef,
30   your illness disperses my sleep
            while others are resting,
and draws me away from tactics and law,

from briefings, and leading the people.
    I'm sick with the service of kings
35   who are ready only for war,
and live for a letter from your right hand,
                with news of your cure.
        Then praise like the crown-
plate on the temple of time will be given,
40 and thanks to Him who has shown me greatness

like sand on the shore
        and the rain from clouds,
and my soul, which was anxious, will sigh.
        Your sickness, my son, is herald—
45   a necklace will honor your bride;
            the boils breaking, a signal—
you'll bear illustrious buds to our people;
        and the whitish spots proclaim—

specks of silver will shine
50 on the bride's dress and your groom's crown
                as your skin presages
        beautiful stitches to cover the cloth
of the canopy; and you'll be lifted,
        like the wounds across your flesh,
55   to power, and onto the council of elders.
So guard your soul as the illness withdraws,

and eat what the doctors prescribe;
        ignore the faithless,
and if you find, with God's grace, health,
60   read and write of the things that amaze you;
for your mind will lift you beyond constellations,
                and raise you higher than rank
        as you rise above your own generation,
in your seeking out newness, the ancient, and hidden;

65   then you'll be, like Joseph, confirmed among brothers,
        and like Asher, blessed above sons.

PASS OF SAND

And when he went out to fight against Osuna and Marur he passed through a place that was full of sand, in the year 4806 [1046], and he had already crossed there in his youth when he fled Cordoba during the great battle, and he said:

Pass of sand,
   have you heard how I passed
     alone and afraid
as I fled through you with my stave?
   Now I cross you with hordes
     who listen to me as a father,
   and wait for my word as for rain,
and look to my thought as a vision;
     and because the Lord my God
has blessed them wherever I've turned,
   they're willingly drawn in my cord.

AMONG MY FRIENDS

And he found, God honor him, that his body and strength were diminishing with age in the battle that took place in the summer of 4814 [1054], and he recited this poem of lament:

Among my friends could I find
  a heart more bitter than mine—
    among my neighbors
  a woman whose wailing is greater,
or someone to grant me the legs of a hind
    to run to the jackals
who'd teach me to mourn for my youth?

After sixty-one years that I've passed
is there left a hair's-breadth space in my soul
    for the singers?
  And now that the sky withholds
    the bright cloud of my boyhood,
will time still shed its dew on my paths?
After the light of my youth has been dimmed

    can I pour as before the choicest
  of oils—in my lamp for a flame?
The graves of my friends have spoken,
  and say I'll join them soon
    to pitch my tent in their world:
      if I can't recover my power,
take up a shovel and start on my tomb.

Aging's grief has set
  in my heart a flaming fire
  whose tongue makes ash of my hair.
Weakness has wakened the pain in my knees,
  and I struggle now even at court,
    on level ground.
I grieve for the soul which is dear to me,

and it's right that one mourns what is dear.
For I've seen as my beard grows white,   30
   a spot on the walls of my heart
      darken with age,
         like soot on a pot.
   If I had time in my power,
      I'd bind it with cord   35

and keep it from lifting a hand to my hair;
and yet, were it only the fire
   of suffering that rose to my head—
     the pain of that heat
would be to me juice from the winepress.   40
But age has drained the youth from my face,
   and now the young women despise me.

Who could help me to be like God
   and know if the day of my death
     were distant or near—   45
when I'll be breathless dust in the grave,
or when from that dust my spirit will rise?
   My heart insists I've long to live.
     If my body grieves,

     may the Lord almighty heal its wounds,   50
may He grant me strength in my weakness,
and power like that of the eagle's wings
     in my limbs, may He sustain me
   in His goodness and mercy.
I put my trust and hope   55
   in the Lord as long as I live.

            • • •

They say "There's rest in the grave,"
    though I fear I'll meet my choices.
Death they call Going on to the Fathers,
   and they're right: 60
       the Fathers are there.
But why when I die will they hurry my corpse
   to the shades of the world below

from the shadow of roof and home,
   and why wrap my flesh in a shroud   65

---

when both in the dirt will decay?
  Why use water to cleanse me
when tomorrow the stench at my waist will pollute me?
  Ages and ages have been on the earth,
70   and I, Lord, am nothing among them.

You sent me out in the world
    before I asked for life,
  and gave me at birth to destruction,
a source of misfortune, a stone to start trouble.
75   You made me fine to behold,
      but soon will alter my form.
    And your actions were righteous

    and your words have been faithful—
  while the breath of mine and my
80   mouth have been snake-like.
Bring me a scroll, and my ink and pen,
    and today I'll inscribe my confession.
Like a freshet my eyes will flow when they read,
    because in the grave there won't be tears,

85   and I'll weep
  for the excellent form my friends
will rush to the place appointed for all,
for the noble form to be covered in dust—
for the dust in its mouth, and over its eyes;
90   and my tongue which has told of my life
      will lie in its box

    like a stone in the heart of the sea;
and my eyes which have witnessed much wonder
    will rot in their sockets,
95   consumed in a hole.
My palate will lose its savor and speech;
    my ears will fail in their hearing;
      my arms and legs will be still.

And, most bitter—like this I'll be called
100   from the grave to justice.
All of my deeds will be weighed in its balance—
    merit to one side, sin to the other.

And maybe an angel will speak for my virtue
    and raise the side of transgression,
        and the side of merit bring down;

he'll remind, in my judgment, the Rock,
of my diligent study of Scripture and Law,
    and I'll hear:
"The Lord in your work has long found favor."
    Then the scales will tilt toward merit,
        and I'll rejoice in my passing
to the great Glory of God which will gather me,

    as it gathers the moon and stars.

RISE EARLY

Rise early and look at the sky
coming on in gold and points of silver,
while darkness's face like a black man flees
    before a pale girl's glare—

and, to the shrieks of birds in the air,
drink from a fawn's outstretched, noble hand
wine whose light in its cup is the sun's,
    its scent like cassia and myrrh.

YOUR YEARS ARE SLEEP

Your years are sleep,
   their fortune's wheel a dream
best, my friend, to shut your
eyes and ears—God
      grant you strength—   5
and leave the hidden things
around you   to one
   who's good with clues.

Bring me wine from a cup
      held by a girl,   10
   who excels on the lute;
a mature vintage, made by Adam,
or new, from Noah's fields.
Its hue like living coral
and gold, its bouquet   15
      like calamus and myrrh—

like David's wine that queens prepared,
impeccably, or graceful harems.
The day it was put in his pitcher,
he sang to Jerimoth's harp   20
      unsurpassingly, saying
this should be sealed and stored
            in casks in the cellar—
for those who drink with excellent hearts

and hold their glasses wisely,   25
and keep the laws of Kohelet,
fearing death,
            and the fury to come.

SAD FRIEND

Sad friend:
Wed
water to the grape vine's fruit
and gather the two
in a cup . . . your mouth
like a bridegroom's
chamber holds them
soon they'll swell in your
head and
suddenly
in your heart give birth to joy.

HOW I HELPED THE WISE

*And he recited a poem in which he boasts and offers an
excellent description of wine:*

Have you heard how I helped the wise,
and the elders on their paths to perfection?
And the God-fearing boys so fine to behold
   and so young,
         and their brothers?   5
I ordered a court prepared for a party
and said: "Let's spend the day sweetly,
we'll drink in honor of the parting-to-come;
   grief awaits each in his halting;

friendship and energy are sisters,   10
   death and departure—twins."
So they came to the cushions threaded with scarlet
         and splendid embroidery
and flasks and bowls full of nuts
   in reach of philanthropists like us;   15
       under the cedars where doves
     flirted, fluttering in pairs,
and the furrows filled with the wine of clouds

and drank and sent forth their secrets.
And we were at ease, hearts   20
       unstubborn and free.
   Then I sent for Jubal's son,
who rushed with his harp and perfect lute,
   and I cradled my flask,
cut like an almond and studded with jewels.   25
   I called for my family, which came
for the vine's son, the vineyard's heir—

in its pitchers deprived of light,
   like Tamar,
   in her widowhood wronged by the law.   30

And the brimming womb they emptied was boneless.
    The vintage prisoner of two
        years in the dark
      heart of the pitcher was free.
35 It had aged, and time worn away at its skin,
though its eye was bright as a boy's blush;

it was fragrant, though not with frankincense,
and seasoned, although without herbs;
    it looked like fire
40   though it poured like water,
and was folly's embodiment, though it gathered the wise;
    it was lightning—with showers to follow:
      not the flash of the false alarm.
They poured it across their bodies by night
45 and went out wise from the cloak of their darkness.

While its glow was imposed
      on the brightness of day,
    they'd winced looking up to the heavens.
And they held it, though it moved their lips—
50 though not by threats
        or strength of arm.
It spoke within them—although it was still,
    and had the guest-list skipping like
      fawns, or gazelles.

55 At once they felt their wisdom flee,
and their knowledge taken captive entirely.
    And their eyes went dim—
      as it addressed the ambassador;
      and frivolity swayed the sages
60   with its richness, bouquet, and savor;
and they hid behind their glasses of onyx,
went redder than rubies in a poor man's hand,
the pitcher's prisoner— like faces gone flush,

    as though it were light
65 which had brushed their temples and stuck.
    They tilted it back, into their throats,
and it rose to the heads of the haughty in power,
and by dusk they were stretching
      out on their sides,

as though hit with a hammer in Yael's hand.   70
At dawn when they woke not a one could rise,
          or raise his head,

as though their feet no longer had toes,
nor their backs
               the spines to prop them.   75
And they said: Who *are* you and What *is* this?
and stirred as though sloughing a dream.
    And I answered:
                    listen to words
which friends and enemies alike will attest to;   80
    and they were heard

in every court and up to the gate
          and heights of the city,
    and no one denies them:
I am the heir of Kehat, the remnant of Merari,   85
    men of renown, and excellent craft—
        and from my father to
          Samuel, Elkanah's son,
             the blood lines cross.
Likewise with Moses, the prophet of God,   90

    who is kin to me.
When the peoples are gathered I'll
call him *my father,*
    and he'll call me *my son.*
    When the peoples are gathered.   95
And they who question my lineage will find
               their own much flawed.
    I have glory and wealth,
though God alone has strength and power;

my songs surpass even those of the Levites,   100
    even those of the close-cropped priests.
    Coffers of gold are within my dominion,
        and chests of the finest clothes.
In my presence the experts go dumb,
and scholars as though they were guilty.   105
    And they leave with their
        lips pressed   together
    when I pass, their eyes are squinted.

They stand there in silence before me—
110   even the movers and shakers;
I reveal to them marvelous things, of hidden interests,
    "obscure"— and fashion my difficult rhymes,
      which know no peer in creation.
      But beyond all this, and better,
115   inasmuch as I'm able
none of my actions are rooted in anger.
If I'm forced to sin, or sin in secret—

may the Lord forgive me my compulsion and lapse.

ROUGE IN APPEARANCE

Rouge in appearance
   and pleasant to drink,
      mixed in Spain
   and prized in Bombay;
weak in its pitcher but rising to the head it
      rules in heads that sway.
Even the mourner whose tears
fall with his heart's blood,
      disperses his grief in retreat with wine.
As though friends—passing the cup from hand to hand—
      were rolling dice, for a diamond.

TAKE THE CRYSTAL

Take the crystal cup from the fawn—
   its grape blood—like fire
      flashing through hail.
Her lips are like threads of scarlet;
the roof of her mouth is excellent wine,
and her talk, like her neck, is perfumed.

From the blood of the slain, the tip of her hand
has reddened: half is like ruby, half like pearl.

From *Ben Mishle*: (After Proverbs)

❧ FROM ELIASSAF'S PREFACE ❦

Said Eliassaf, the son of our Teacher, Shmuel HaLevi, may His Rock
Protect Him: After giving thanks to Him whom it is proper to thank, the
Lord, whom nothing preceded and whom nothing will follow, and after
confessing that He is the single most glorious God of all tongues and
every place, and that He is the source of all degrees and measure of
goodness, I gathered in this book—which is the fruit of the labor of my
father and master, may he please God—epigrams and parables. My father
called this book *Ben Mishle* [After Proverbs], and I began copying and
studying it while I was just a little past six years of age, this having been
calculated from the hour of my birth, which was—as precisely recorded
by one who made note at the time—at the midpoint of the seventh hour
of the first day of the week, on the morning of the 23rd of Marheshvan in
the year 4810 since the creation of the world, and the morning of the 23rd
of Jomada I, in the year 441 after the Hejira [1049 CE]. And it was my father
who instructed me to gather and arrange this material in alphabetical
order. All of it is elegantly crafted with balanced meters and well-chosen
subjects and words, the foundations and ideas of which were taken from
the epigrams of the various nations and diverse peoples, which are found
within their books and heard on their lips, on those of the learned and the
people alike, together with those of his own invention, to which his talent
and occasion gave rise. At times there will be found in it contradictory
things for mysterious reasons, which will be revealed to the reader if he
possesses a sharp mind and uses his intellect, and repetitions to empha-
size a matter or to make something clear or to ornament a parable, as is
the case with the parables found in the books of authors like him, and
even in our sacred books, which are the word of the Lord, may He be
blessed, and His expression, and the collections of our prophets, God's
blessing be upon them, because indeed, nothing seems beautiful unless it
has an opposing aspect, and sometimes both are beautiful at one time but
not at another, or in one manner but not in another. And he gave the
book the following verses as a motto:

> Take excellent lessons and place your mind
>   on *Ben Mishle* of Shmuel HaNagid.
> The man who waits at its gate won't err;
> he'll be upright in word and faith and deed.

TRUTH IS HARD

Truth is hard,
    the end sudden,
  and justice like wisdom
    distant and generous.

Tack your heart by them on the way
which twists with the sky-dweller's will.

WHEN THE LORD IS WITH YOU

When the Lord is with you,
    sit at home:
you can hunt your beasts and birds from there.

The wretched will labor but never be full,
    then vomit their meals—
    and choke on their words.

ONE WHO WORKS AND BUYS
HIMSELF BOOKS

One who works
    and buys himself books,
while his heart inside them
    is vain or corrupt

resembles a cripple
    who draws on the wall
a hundred legs,
        then can't get up.

HOW COULD YOU LOATHE

How could you loathe
        someone who holds
your sins against you and your heart?

No one will hold you
        more to the truth
than a friend whom you've weakened and hurt.

FORGIVE THE MAN WHO SINNED
AGAINST YOU

Forgive the man who sinned against you
   often—just when revenge would be sweet;
and in your heart don't loathe the ugly—
   in the harvest's refuse, there's chaff and wheat.

IF YOU'RE FINDING THE
GOOD AT FAULT

If you're finding the good at fault,
   you're in the dark all alone;
if you can't see the kindness of others,
   there isn't much hope for your own.

DELAY YOUR SPEECH

Delay your speech
  if you want your words
to be straight and free of deceit—

as a master archer
    is slow to take aim
while splitting a grain of wheat.

I'D SUCK BITTER POISON FROM
THE VIPER'S MOUTH

I'd suck bitter poison from the viper's mouth
and live by the basilisk's hole forever,
rather than suffer through evenings with boors,
fighting for crumbs from their table.

IF YOU DON'T HAVE THE
POWER TO PAY

If you don't have the power to pay back the cruel,
    forget what they did (while you hurt) to your image;
but perhaps you're a hero and *can* get revenge:
      then atone for their sins with your courage.

HE WHO LINGERS AT THE COURT
OF THE KING

He who lingers at the court of the king
and puts up with the ministers' stomping and noise,
and isn't provoked by the scandal he sees,
    and oils his words—

    finds his way eased when he leaves.

IN BUSINESS DON'T GET INVOLVED

In business, don't get involved
   with a man who tells all he knows;
if he can't keep track of a word,
   how could you trust him with gold?

IF YOU SHAME A MAN

If you shame a man for the flaws he shows you
    but keeps well-hidden from others,
how could your heart not likewise disgrace you
    for the flaws of your own that you'd smother?

PEOPLE WELCOME THE RICH

People welcome the rich
    with deference, respect, and credit,
but scorn the poor and charge them
    with crimes they didn't commit.

HE WHOSE HEART IN HIS HEART

He whose heart
  in his heart is raised,
although—in public—
    he isn't well known

the Lord lifts
  in invisible ways,
as others will
    when they're shown.

IF YOU LEAVE A LONG-LOVED FRIEND

If you leave a
   long-loved friend
      today in disgust,

you'll be like a man
   destroying a building
      that took him a year

   to raise from dust.

RESPECT AND DISCRETION

Respect and discretion
　　will bring you wealth
and lead the way on
　　to power—

but one who's quick
　　to air out his thoughts
will meet disappointment
　　and sour.

THE RICH ARE SMALL

The rich are small in number
  and the brilliant likewise are few;
and the number of each is further reduced
    when they step side by side into view.

YOU WHO'D BE WISE

You who'd be wise
should inquire
   into the nature of
     justice and evil

from your teachers,
seekers like yourself,
   and the students
who question your answer.

WHEN YOU'RE DESPERATE

When you're desperate ride
        the lion's back
      to sustenance,
but don't use others
      or envy them—

the envy will weigh on
your heart, not theirs.

IT'S HEART THAT DISCERNS

It's heart that discerns
   between evil and good,
so work to develop your heart.

How many are there
   who heartless destroy,
and think their destruction a start?

STAB YOUR HEART

Stab your heart with the arrow of study
    when your soul tires of learning, and learn
that the fastest horse receives the whip,
    and the strongest oxen—goads that burn.

IS THERE ANY FRUSTRATION

Is there any frustration like that of these:
   the wise being judged by fools,
failing strength as it's broken by force,
    or the kind who depend on the cruel?

DID YOUR FATHER LEAVE YOU GLORY

Did your father leave you glory then die?
Extend and perfect his line.

If not—build for your soul on your own.
Be a father for those to come.

H

COULD KINGS RIGHT A PEOPLE
GONE BAD

Could kings right a people gone bad,
   while they themselves are twisted?
How, in the woods, could shadows that bend
   be straight when the trees are crooked?

THE KING

The king's fickleness
  resembles the drunk's:
what should anger him pleases—
  what should please, he debunks.

He'll praise the excellent,
  then disdain it twice,
rewarding his hacks
  for double the price.

HE'LL BRING YOU TROUBLE

He'll bring you trouble with talk like dreams,
   invoking song and verse to cheat you;
but dreams, my son, aren't what they seem:
   not all the poet says is true.

THE WISE UNDERSTAND

The wise understand the maker of parables,
   without exerting much strength,
but the fool won't fathom his slightest,
   until you've explained it at length.

ASSISTANTS COME TO JUDGMENT
IN GROUPS

Assistants come to judgment in groups,
　　but rulers won't gather in pairs by the gate:
many, like arrows, are found in a quiver
　　while the sword lies alone in its sheath.

THE GOOD STUDENTS TEND

The good students tend
 to doubt mysteries;
the foolish—what's obvious.

And the skillful singer
 from the well of reason
draws wonder on the rope of his hunch.

WHAT'S FAMILIAR IS SOMETIMES DISTANCED

What's familiar is sometimes distanced,
    and the distanced sometimes brought near:
and the cavalier rider in fetlock-deep water
    who falls finds it up to his ears.

THE HEART HOLDS HIDDEN
KNOWLEDGE

The heart holds hidden
   knowledge,
and with words of its language
in your wisdom you'll find it—

like a book that was written
   by an inept hand,
and went unread,
until a sage looked through it

   and saw what it said.

FIRST WAR

First war resembles
   a beautiful mouth we
all want to flirt with
   and believe—.

Later it's more
   a repulsive old whore
whose callers are bitter
   and grieve.

SOAR, DON'T SETTLE

Soar, don't settle for earth
   and sky—soar to Orion;
and be strong, but not like an ox or mule
   that's driven—strong like a lion.

COMMERCE HAS MARKETS

Commerce has markets,
and the council of the learned
is a market to Law.
The bazaars
hold many merchants,
who settle on a price
for every jewel.

THREE THINGS

All who'd live by risk
and resistance manage
   three things:

high-sea commerce,
   excellent enemies,
and the company of kings.

THE FOOLISH ENEMY'S FACE
TELLS ALL

The foolish enemy's face tells all—
　　but the clever's deceives and offers you smiles,
and talks as though his heart were with yours,
　　and acts like your friend or your child.

MAN'S WISDOM IS IN WHAT
HE WRITES

Man's wisdom is in what he writes,
good sense at the end of his pen;
and using his pen he can climb to the height
   of the scepter in the hand of his king.

From *Ben Kohelet*: (After Ecclesiastes)

If you'd like to know the world of the future,
consider Ben Kohelet at length—
and know that time won't ever be killed
with great advice, or with strength.

GAZING THROUGH THE NIGHT

Gazing through the
      night and its stars,

   or the grass and its bugs,

I know in my heart these swarms
are the craft of surpassing wisdom.   5

   Think: the skies
      resemble a tent,
    stretched taut by loops
and hooks;

and the moon with its stars,   10
  a shepherdess,
    on a meadow
      grazing her flock;

and the crescent hull in the looser clouds

   looks like a ship being tossed;   15

    a whiter cloud, a girl
      in her garden
        tending her shrubs;

and the dew coming down is her sister
      shaking water   20
    from her hair onto the path;

  as we
    settle in our lives,

like beasts in their ample stalls—

  fleeing our terror of death,   25
    like a dove
      its hawk in flight—

though we'll lie in the end like a plate,
    hammered into dust and shards.

LOVERS OF LIFE

Lovers of life on earth,
   know what you do is profound:
you're spliced from the root of death,
   and branches return to the ground.

THE MULTIPLE TROUBLES OF MAN

> The multiple troubles of man,
>   my brother, like slander and pain,
> amaze you? Consider the heart
>   which holds them all
> in strangeness, and doesn't break.

BE GLAD, SHE SAID

"Be glad," she said,
  "God brought you
  to fifty years
    in your world"—
but didn't know there's
    no division
    between, as I see it,
my days that have passed
and Noah's
    of which I've heard.
In the world I have nothing
but the hour I'm in,
  which stands for a moment
and then like a cloud moves on.

EARTH TO MAN

Earth to man
   is a prison forever.

These tidbits, then,
   for fools:

Run where you will.
   Heaven surrounds you.
     Get out if you can.

YOUR LOVED ONES DEPRESS YOU

Your loved ones depress you
with debt and transgression
and your friends remind you
of all your flaws;

so think of the sins you
hold within you,
as each destroys
your worthiest cause.

Your soul will struggle
forever—take care.
And don't entice it
in secret:

the Lord sees all.

SOUL OPENS INSIDE YOU

Soul opens inside you on beauty—
then tells you to seek in the world
    and ignore its flaws.

Heart says: you'll live forever—
and death as it speaks
    grasps you with claws.

H

THE CHILD AT ONE OR TWO

The child at one or two
   crawls like a snake on the floor;
and at ten he skips to his father,
   like a kid among goats on the hills;

5   at twenty, love in his heart
   takes hold—and he struts for girls;
he basks in the glories of youth
   for his pride and power, at thirty;

reaching forty he ripens,
10   and joins the elders, his friends;
at fifty the sleep of his youth
   in whiteness is brought to an end;

and the terrors of time assault him,
   when a man passes sixty;
15   till seventy then he sighs
   with age, and seems to be saintly;

but time surrounds him at eighty,
   trapped in the fowler's snare;
and at ninety he can't distinguish
20   between the plough and scythe;

at a hundred—who gets to a hundred?—
   men in amazement approach him;
when he dies he lies with maggots,
   repulsive to one and all;

25   so it's right that I wax elegiac
   from time to time in my soul.

FEAR FIVE TO THE POWER OF FIVE

Fear five to the power of five:
illustrious youth growing old,
spats turning hostile with friends,

retribution for each transgression,
achievement finding misfortune,
and armies erased in the end.

I QUARTERED THE TROOPS
FOR THE NIGHT

I quartered the troops for the night in a fortress
    which soldiers destroyed long ago,
and they fell asleep at its walls and foundations
    while beneath us its masters slept on.

5   And I wondered: what had become
    of the people who dwelled here before us?
Where were the builders and soldiers, the wealthy
    and poor, the slaves and their lords?

the bereaved and the women in labor; the sons
10   and their fathers; the mourners and grooms?
Great nations had come in succession
    in the course of months and years,

and they settled across the back of the earth,
    but rest in the heart of the ground—
15   their magnificent palaces turned into tombs,
    their pleasant courts to dust,

and if they could lift their heads and emerge,
    they'd take our lives and pleasure.
In truth, my soul, in truth and soon,
20   I'll be like them—and these sleepers.

WHY REPEAT THE SINS

Why repeat the sins
    you know will make you sad
and not hold back from sinning
        for sorrow—

like a dove whose brood was slaughtered
    in the nest, and yet returns
        over and over again
            until she's taken?

TIME DEFIES AND BETRAYS
THE PATRICIANS

Time defies and betrays the patricians,
 and drives all who grow proud;
and lengthens the maverick's wandering,
 and separates twins, like a shroud.

YOU FELT THE FEAR OF DEATH

You felt the fear of death
when his being gave out and he died;
and you moped around by his grave,
and forgot the grave in time.

WHY SHOULD THE HEARTS
OF YOU PURISTS

Why should the hearts of you purists bear
  the grief you fear, yet may not follow?

There'll be more than more than enough to withstand
  when the heart discovers its sorrow.

LUXURIES EASE

Luxuries ease, but when trouble comes
people are plagued for the wealth they've accrued.
    The peacock's tail is spectacular—
but it weighs him down on the day he's pursued.

YOU'RE TRAPPED, MY TONGUE

You're trapped, my tongue, and bound
in my throat, and doors conceal you.
So how do you issue your arrow-like speech,
   your words like spears that kill?

   How, from a pit so deep,
how do you bring the innocent down?
You have no balm except for the worm,
which eats through the grave as you sleep.

FRIENDS, A FENCE SURROUNDS US

Friends, a fence surrounds us,
   and spheres through which we'll never drill;
and we're like the yolk in an egg and its white;
   and the world is our shell.

You think there'll be refuge from evil,
   but there isn't any way out:
What could we do that God hasn't done—
   or even consider—

   while we're being devout?

YOUTH BRINGS US

Youth brings us toward three things:
  memory, caution, and mind.
And age always brings on in exchange:
  oblivion, folly, decline.

HE WHO DEPENDS ON THE PRINCES

He who depends on the princes
  rises and falls with their fate;
as he who fleeing by ship is saved
  from evil, or sinks with its weight.

ON THEIR COUCHES STRETCHED OUT
AT THE TREASURY

On their couches stretched out at the treasury,
where vigilance should know no relief,
you fell asleep without fear by the window
and time came through like a thief.

COME UP AND SEE THE COURT

Come up and see the court of the patron
    you used to frequent, where goats now camp.
There remains neither door nor threshold within it,
    nor dog to water its wall with scent.

SUFFER THE WORLD

Suffer the world you're trapped in,
   and your soul which is trapped in your flesh,
through fertile thinking, barren cunning,
   and intrigue's impotent mesh.

THE MARKET

I crossed through a souk where the butchers
hung oxen and sheep at their sides,
there were birds and herds of fatlings like squid,
their terror loud
as blood congealed over blood   5
and slaughterers' knives opened veins.

In booths alongside them the fishmongers,
and fish in heaps, and tackle like sand;
and beside them the Street of the Bakers
—whose ovens are fired through dawn.   10

They bake, they eat, they lead their prey;
they split what's left to bring home.

•

And my heart understood how they did it and asked:
Who are you to survive?
What separates you from these beasts,   15
which were born and knew waking and labor and rest?
If they hadn't been given by God for your meals,
they'd be free.
If He wanted this instant
He'd easily put you in their place.   20

They've breath, like you, and hearts,
which scatter them over the earth;
there was never a time when the living didn't die,
nor the young that they bear not give birth.

Pay attention to this, you pure ones,   25
and princes so calm in your fame,
know if you'd fathom the worlds of the hidden:
THIS IS THE LAW OF MAN.

FLUTTER OR REST

Flutter or rest, every soul
   in goodness receives its lot:
to this one much, to another a little,
   guile won't change what you've got.

SEE THE FRAUD FLOW BY

See the fraud flow by like water—
slowly, like fire glowing with flame.
 Time undoes what secrets accomplish,
like spies when seen who play the friend.

THE EARTHQUAKE

*And he recited this poem in which he describes an earthquake that took
place in the city in the year 1047, and there was great fear since
there had been nothing like it and homes were destroyed
and the walls gave way and many people nearly died:*

My Shepherd, I'm still where I lie
   and look out over your greatness;
      my mouth speaks of your miracles,
my tongue gives voice to your marvelous acts.
⁵   Over the earth's place and foundation
         your hand has ruled:
      you've crushed the groves in season,
the vineyard's fruit, the fig in flower.

How could a person sin when he sees
¹⁰   the contortions of each man's journey?
      God to the godless delivers him
and casts him into a wicked man's hand.
You drive the soul like a leaf from its vine,
   as the harp is thrummed you drive it,
¹⁵   and march across the earth's back,
         then fold it up like a robe.

He when He pleases who brings out the sun
   and lights the hills with fire,
      ripples the mountains like wind
²⁰   rippling spikes of wheat in a field.
He causes the land to skip like a calf,
   it raced like a wild young ox;
      His wrath twists the foundations
like hikers through rugged terrain.

²⁵   I heard it—and my stomach churned;
   at the voice of the rushing I struggled.
      Remembering now how it happened

my heart balks and I tremble:
You rose by dark to shake the earth
   in the blackness of night and the gloom,   30
you turned the land on its head like a bowl,
     and its peaks beneath us buckled.

He who remembers the fear of that night
   grows weary of life in his soul;
      it gathered a terror so great   35
   the highest among us were humbled.
"Twice, yea thrice," God touched the earth,
   and, like a drunkard it toppled.
      The quake shook like a troop
spreading out in its raid on a city—   40

and hearts gave way as it whitened the hair
   of women whose hearts were young;
      and the pillars of heaven weakened,
the foundations of earth were destroyed;
   its walls pressed up on each other,   45
        the highest tower came down,
     and all the dwellings were shaken:
they trembled in fear of the Lord.

Buildings anchored firmly in earth
   weren't spared from destruction;   50
the city's walls were brought to the ground,
     stricken—like beaten olives.
Infants nursing slipped from their mothers
   and groped for their weakened grasp;
they were scared, and didn't know what to do.   55
The righteous woman was one with the shrew.

The sound of rupture came from the roofs
   like a woman clawing her flesh,
   mourning the loss of her only son.
Home collapsed on neighboring home,   60
acacia and cedar fell at their roots;
   the townspeople wallowed in earth
   like a sword swaddled in cloth,
and every standing thing bowed down.

Servants fell onto bedding they straightened;   65
   the faces of all the king's daughters

deep in their chambers were covered in fear;
hearts with labor were straining
    like mothers bearing their sons;
70   and the soul of each man inside him
            tossed like a ship on the waves,
as the men huddled in terrified crowds

confessing their sins, and saying:
"So the Lord's congregation is judged
75   which didn't do justice
to the afflicted and poor; it sated itself—
grew coarse in its being and fat in its soul;
grew thick and fat and kicked at the Lord."
        Then we said: "Our end has come,
80   and destruction's hand now sweeps the world."

It moved from west to east,
    it didn't swerve from its path.
It gave us to drink from the waters of ruin
    and fed us its stew of death.
85   And then—after He'd crushed it,
            He steadied the earth
to leave us a name and a remnant,
    to save us for a great deliverance.

He bound the people in a circle of joy,
90   and stripped off their jacket of fear.
All through the night their song was heard,
and thanks for the people's deliverance—
    for salvation and the robe of justice
        the hand of the Lord had bestowed.
95   May you always lift a hand
        high to redeem us with mercy, our Rock!

Lord who floats the land over sea,
who stretches the north over empty space
    and hangs the earth on nothingness,
100   you've given sentence
            to be heard from the heavens:
        the earth feared and grew still.
You shook the earth and cleft it:
    now heal its wound, for it totters.

TWO ECLIPSES

And at the end of the month of Kislev in the year 1044 he composed
a poem in which he told of two eclipses, solar and lunar, which
took place in the aforesaid month. And he announced that there
would be a total lunar eclipse, the longest of its day, in the
middle of the month of Iyyar, of the same year.

My friend, are you sleeping?
Rise and wake the dawn,
   look up at the sky
like a leopard skin stippled above us
and see the moon where it should be full,   5
    go dark like a kettle, or kiln,
  like the face of a girl—
    half of it flushed,
  the other darkened in shadow.
    Return and glance at the sun,   10
brought to the end of the month in dimness,
  its halo of light on the darkness,
like a crown on the head of a Libyan princess,
  and the earth whose sun has set,
    reddened—as though with tears.   15

Both of the beacons were stricken
    in the space of a single month
by Him whose dominion is splendor and strength;
He covered the moon with His circle of earth,
    and the sun with His moon: 20
this is the work of the Lord who toys with creation.

  He fashioned patches of dark in the moon,
    and the sun He created clear,
  therefore I liken them now
in their dimness against the dark,   25
    to women bereaved:
      the face of the one is bruised,
    the other both bruised and wounded—

the light of day on a day gone dim,
30 and the light of night darkened at evening
during the watch.
Like an angry king who brings trouble
on his lords in their own domains,
first He struck the brightness of night,
35 and afterwards blotted the daylight,
like a king who prepared a poisonous cup
for his mistress, and then for his queen.
Behold what happened—look closely in wonder,
study it well, and read:

40 Yours is the greatness,
who brought the light in its weight and measure,
and darkened the moon at its cycle's center,
like a bird caught in a snare.
You'll do it again in five months more;
45 looking onto the earth,
you'll make it reel like a drunkard.
You've ordered the moth and it eats
the Bear and Orion in great constellation;
you fixed for the living among them
50 a place like a shield;
and all when you rule will be trodden as one,
though not with a shout in a winepress.

Yours is the glory, yours entire,
every horse and chariot houghed.
55 It's you who brings on heat in winter,
and winter, at summer's height;
you who upends the abyss,
who brings affliction into the sea
like a woman in labor;
60 you who'll cast toward all the living—death,
as the arrow flies to its target;
you on the bitter and great
and terrible day of judgment
who will wake me and judge
65 all who've forsaken the statues,
commandments, and Law.

When you place my deeds in judgment's scale,
may the side of evil, lighter, rise.

———————

On the day you lift me up from my dust
I'll turn and my spirit in fear of your wrath
        will flee, and you'll say:
"Peace be upon you; be still, and do not fear."

If there remains not a trace of my righteousness,
        may your mercy be near.

THE TYRANT WHO RULES THE
HOMELESS AND POOR

The tyrant who rules the homeless and poor
with harshness forgets, enticed by his power,
that the Lord holds moments like arrows that kill—
and one will soon strike through his liver.

MY SPIRIT

My spirit on which, after God, I lean,
    and care for with all my labor—
after these fifty long years together,
    why would you turn and run?

THE BLACK OF MY HAIR

The black of my hair has gone white,
and time has bent my back which had been like an "i"
    into a "p,"
            and twisted

  both of my legs like the leg of a "t."

ASK THE DEAD AND THEY'LL
TELL YOU

Ask the dead and they'll tell you: Come
look at your vitae's secret and sins;
   why insist that you have no creator—
while your mouth says "liar" through all your limbs?

SEND THE LORD TO THE PEOPLE

Send the Lord to the people
  who dwell in darkness;
they who've been brought to the shadow
    of death by dimness;

and set Him beside the window to watch—
to stand there and spy through the lattice.

CAST YOUR BREAD

Cast your bread for it's good to give
and he whose hand is open will thrive—
lest, in the end, the days deceive you
and strip you of all you've denied.

KNOW OF THE LIMBS

Know of the limbs embroidered with dust
and covered with ashen skin,
and in these graves see the power of kings
reduced to the powder of bone.

You whose souls on earth were exalted,
will soon rise over all—
and be remembered in the world ever after
as a dream as it fades is recalled.

YOU MOCK ME NOW IN YOUR YOUTH

You mock me now in your youth
    because I've grown old and gray;
I'm old, but I've seen the carpenters
    building their coffins for boys.

YOU THINK THERE'S NO HELL
THAT WILL HOLD YOU

You think there's no hell that will hold you
    and run around like a foal,
but the end of all that's in motion is rest,
    of rains and their rivers—a hole.

YOU LOOK THROUGH OPEN EYES

You look through open eyes
    but your heart is fast asleep,
and you fear the wrath of the Lord
    and your heart's transgression is deep.

EVERYTHING HIDDEN

Everything hidden you know and explain,
but the gist of your time from your wisdom is lost:
the moment you think of all that you've been through
   you seem like a dream from the past.

Then why, when a new day comes, are you glad
with your child's delight in the world?

❧ NOTES ❧

IN THE NOTES that follow I try to offer an X ray of the poetry, one that might expose for readers at least something of the complex effect the poems probably had on their eleventh-century audience. References to biblical inlays, or *shibbutsim*, are indicated, though not always quoted in full, since doing so would mislead and provide countless new problems for readers and translator alike. In providing such skeletal indications as "Cf. Leviticus 36:7" I do not mean to suggest that readers look up every citation; rather, I want these references to give readers a sense of the poetry's relation to Scripture, a relation so integral to its worldview and so alien, for the most part, to our own. I quote in full when the quotation is directly relevant in translation, and when the material is drawn from Rabbinic texts that are less accessible to contemporary readers. The poems can and should be read without these notes as well.

It is important here to reiterate that these references, for the most part, reflect linguistic ornamentation rather than full-fledged literary allusion. The latter is occasionally employed, but these notes make no distinction between the "neutral" use of the biblical vocabulary and the variety of more thematic or literary usages. "We might think of the poem," writes Neil Kozody, in one of the more effective descriptions of the *shibbuts* that I have come across, "as a garment woven with great skill from costly and colorful material. Into this fabric have been twined threads of pure gold, beaten down from a single bar, the Bible; . . . They call attention to themselves, first, inviting us to hold up the work, tilting it at a variety of angles and planes in an attempt to perceive whether they might not form some hidden pattern. At the same time, they impart real depth and brilliance to the surfaces surrounding them, and as we study those surfaces we become struck by the impression of motion, as the presence of the pure gold subtly alters the values and intensities of the surrounding hues."

The other literary relationship these notes trace is between HaNagid's verse and its Arabic models. The parallels offered below are, however, only arrows pointing in the direction of that extensive influence. Unless otherwise indicated, translations of Arabic poems are my own, from the Hebrew versions that appear in the articles and books listed in the bibliography (cf. Ratzhaby, Levin, and others).

All citations from the Babylonian Talmud are offered in the Soncino Press translation. Biblical citations most often use the Jewish Publication Society 1917 translation, though the ASV (which it resembles), the 1985 JPS, and other translations have also been consulted.

Ben Tehillim

The 222 poems of *Ben Tehillim* are arranged by editor Dov Yarden into ten groups: battle poems, poems of friendship and praise, poems of wit, elegies and poems of condolence, nature poems, light verse, wine songs, love poems, prayers, and miscellaneous poems. (In Sassoon's edition the work was organized into two categories, reflecting Yehosef's editing and the sixteenth-century manuscript Sassoon worked from: short poems of diverse meters, and longer poems.) The poems are written in a variety of quantitative meters and nearly all maintain a single end rhyme throughout. They were originally copied out by HaNagid's son Yehosef, who has also added the italicized superscriptions to the poems, possibly as dictated by his father.

The order of the present selection has been determined by the translator.

ON FLEEING HIS CITY (67—in the Yarden edition)

"On leaving Cordoba"—HaNagid fled the battle of 1013 when, after three years of ethnic unrest in the region, Berbers under the leadership of Sulayman al-Mustai'in stormed the city and massacred its population, including some sixty scholars. For all practical purposes, this marked the end of the period of the caliphate and its centralized power in Andalusia, though the last caliph was not banished until the Cordovan revolt of 1031. Moshe Ibn Ezra described the situation in his *Book of Remembrance and Discussion*: "[In 1013] there followed in Spain a terrible war the like of which had never been known and which at the end of the century concerned was called the Berber War. It was a time of suffering and misfortune; starvation and want were rampant in the cities, doom knocked at the gates of the government and smote Cordova, the capital. The city suffered many visitations and finally was destroyed or as good as destroyed. There was a decline of all science for no scholars were left, and people were absorbed by their worries" (trans. Schirmann).

The poem is addressed to a friend HaNagid is forced to leave, and it loosely follows many of the conventions of a classical Arabic qasida, including the remembrance of the beloved, a wandering across the "desert," and a final boast. The interested reader might find it instructive to compare the poem to some of its Arabic precursors, particularly, the "Lammiya" (the 'l'-rhymed qasida) of Shanfa'ra (in Michael Sells's *Desert Tracings*), which treats a similar ambition to greatness, albeit in a different tone. See also James Monroe's *Hispano-Arabic Poetry* for Ibn Shuhaid's poems about the same civil war.

HaNagid eventually made his way from Cordoba to Malaga, normally a four-day journey of some ninety miles to the southeast, but probably double that in this instance, since it was unlikely that HaNagid would have used the main roads. We also know from poem 19 ("Pass of Sand") that HaNagid took an indirect route, as the superscription mentions Ecija, Osuna, and Morón, all of which are southwest of Cordoba. Malaga (directly to the south) was safe because it was ruled by a Slavic governor who had made a pact with the Berbers.

Lines 1–2: Literally, "Soul from that which it desires is cut off, and soul from that which it wants is blocked." The verb in the first line of the Hebrew has two variant readings. Yarden reads *geruah* (deriving it from Exodus 5:8, "ye shall not *diminish* aught thereof"); Schirmann reads *geduah*—cut down, or distanced. My somewhat free translation reflects Schirmann's text.

3–4: Cf. Deuteronomy 31:20; Isaiah 30:23: "And He will give the rain for thy seed, wherewith thy sowest the ground, and bread of the increase of the ground, and it shall be fat and plenteous. In that day shall thy cattle feed in large pastures."

4–5: "Precious being" in the original reads literally, "honorable soul." Cf. Ecclesiastes 6:7: "All the labor of man is for his mouth, and yet the appetite is not filled." *Ecclesiastes Rabbah* 6:6: "And yet the appetite [soul/gullet] is not filled . . .

To what may this be likened, to a villager who married a princess. If he brings her everything in the world, they won't matter to her at all. Why? Because she's the princess. So it is with the soul. If you bring it all sorts of worldly delights, they mean nothing to it. Why? Because it is from the most high."

Bernard Septimus comments that the longing in the poem is neither religious nor philosophical so much as aristocratic or high-minded. He compares it to the Aristotelian notion in the *Ethics* (1123a–1125b): "A person seems to be magnanimous in thinking himself worthy of great things when he is worthy. . . . If a man deems himself deserving of great things—especially of the greatest things—when he deserves them, then he will be concerned with one particular object. He is said to be deserving in reference to the external goods. But we place that external good highest which we attribute to the gods, which is deserved most of all by prominent men and is the reward for virtuous action. Such a good is honor, for it is the best of all external goods. Therefore, the magnanimous man will manage honor and dishonor in a manner which is fitting."

9: "pulse of man's flesh"—literally, "flesh of man's flesh."

12–15: The Hebrew here has an intricate weave, picking up on the sound *(ra'ah)* at the end of line 3 in the original. The roots involved in this sound can mean either evil/trouble, or companion/friend. The Hebrew reads: "VeHanefesh b'Ra'ah!/VeYesh Re'im Meree'im." The English weaves "f," "fr," and a grammatical play on "thinking" to mirror the effect of the Hebrew "ra" and the syntax of the original.

13–14: Literally, "Big bodies of faulty (or little) wisdom."

19: Cf. Jeremiah 4:30: "That thou enlargest thine eyes with paint . . . In vain dost thou make thyself fair." The original reads, "the paint of night."

20: Cf. Job 34:35: "Job speaketh without knowledge, and his words are without discernment."

22: Cf. Deuteronomy 14:7.

23–25: The Hebrew contains a play on the words for "white" (as in purity or innocence) and "moon," which in Hebrew are both *levanah*. So the line might also read as follows: "Should someone whose soul is white [or "a moon," or "moonlike"], hold back from longing toward heights like the moon?"

27: Literally, "weaving its wing." Yarden understands, "wings of light." Cf. Psalms 139:9.

29–31: Cf. 1 Kings 10:7, "And behold . . . thou hast wisdom and prosperity exceeding the fame which I heard"; 2 Chronicles 9:5–6.

37: Cf. The Passover Haggadah: "If he had only split the sea for us. . . ," from the Seder song, *Dayenu*, a hymn that dates to the second century BCE.

38: The Hebrew is unclear. Yarden understands the line to read: "with every twisting swimmer [sail]." My reading in this case is based on Schirmann's text, which says: "and split the sea and every twisted trench."

39–40: Literally, "and sail [roam] in ascent to the peak, which only eternity knows."

44–46: Cf. Exodus 21:5–6. Literally, "And I will bore with an awl through the ear of free men [they will choose to be faithful to me out of love], and as for me an ear to my friends will be pierced."

47: Literally, "and for me soul will hold fast to friends, and for me soul will avoid obstructers." Here and in the following lines the English collapses several of the Hebrew lines and the rendering is free.

49–53: Cf. Esther 3:12; Song of Songs 8:7; Exodus 39:6: "And they wrought the onyx stones, inclosed in settings of gold, graven with the engravings of a signet"; Psalms 68:14; Jeremiah 22:14: "'I will build me a wide house and spacious chambers,' and cutteth him out windows, and it is sealed with cedar and painted with vermilion." Literally, "To you who holds a garden bed full of friendship, planted by the river of love, friendship is guarded from youth, and fixed like a seal in wax, like graven gold in the window, on the threshold [or sill] of the temple cut."

54–55: These lines are in some dispute. They might also be read: "May God be with you as your love, and your soul which He loves will deliver you from distress." In line 55 Schirmann reads: "your soul which God loves." Yarden reads: "your soul which I love." Cf. Job 33:24.

56–57: Psalms 68:21: "God is unto us a god of deliverance."

58: Literally, "Until the moon and sun are no more . . ." i.e., forever. Cf. Psalms 72:7: "In his days let the righteous flourish, and abundance of peace til the moon be no more."

Tova Rosen-Moked calls this "in many respects the strangest poem in the diwan . . . and in medieval Hebrew poetry at large." She argues that the poem reflects the conventions of a typical medieval poem about a "fantastic voyage" rather than a simple representation of the poet's experience. HaNagid may, however, have taken such a trip in his youth. In particular, Rosen-Moked suggests that HaNagid drew from *The Seven Voyages of Sinbad* or something like it.

Some scholars feel that HaNagid's journey occurred while he was still a student in Cordoba, possibly as part of a business apprenticeship; others suggest that it makes more sense to place the poem and its events later in the diwan, after HaNagid's arrival in the port city of Malaga (population 15–20,000), where he set up shop as a trader, or "spice merchant," in 1013.

Line 1: Cf. Leviticus 26:36–7: "I will send a faintness into their heart in the lands of their enemies; and the sound of a driven leaf shall chase them; and they shall flee as one fleeth from the sword; and they shall fall when none pursueth."

3: Literally, "for my foot when it slips is there a getting up?" Cf. Psalms 38:17: "When my foot slippeth, they magnify themselves against me"; 2 Samuel 22:37; Psalms 18:37.

5–8: Cf. Amos 6:8. The meaning of these lines in the Hebrew is uncertain, and Yarden and Schirmann differ in their readings here. Schirmann reads: "By my soul, the All [God] will come to help and comfort the afflicted soul. By their souls, there is none who would come on the day of my confusion, and they saw me confused." The translation reflects Yarden's text.

10: Cf. Ezekiel 29:11–12: "And I will make the land of Egypt desolate in the midst of the countries that are desolate, and her cities among the cities that are laid waste shall be desolate forty years."

11: Cf. 1 Samuel 2:8: "He raiseth up the poor out of the dust"; Psalms 113:7; Isaiah 25:12: "And the high fortress of thy walls will He bring down . . . and bring to the ground, even to the dust."

15–16: Cf. *Sepher Yetzirah 8:* "Keep your mouth from speaking and your heart from its speculation."

17–18: Cf. Proverbs 24:21; Isaiah 33:15: "That stoppeth his ears from hearing of blood, and shutteth his eyes from looking at evil."

19–20: Cf. 1 Samuel 2:12–34; Numbers 25; Genesis 38:8–10.

21–22: Cf. Deuteronomy 6:7: "And when thou walkest by the way and when thou liest down and when thou risest up." From the daily liturgy, the *Shema*.

23–24: Cf. Numbers 22:3: "And Moab was overcome with dread"; Psalms 22:24: "Ye that fear the Lord, praise him; . . and stand in awe of Him, all ye the seed of Israel"; Deuteronomy 32:27, 1:17; 1 Samuel 18:15; Job 41:17, 19:29.

25–26: Cf. Koran 112:3: "In the Name of God, the Merciful, the Compassionate, Say: He is God, One God, the Everlasting Refuge, who has not begotten, and has not been begotten, and equal to Him is not anyone" (Arberry translation).

33–34: Cf. Ezekiel 27:6.

37: Cf. Job 20:17: "He shall not look upon the rivers, the flowing streams of honey and curd." JPS (1988) has "the rivers of honey, the brooks of cream." Job 29:6: "When my steps were washed with butter, and the Rock poured me out rivers of oil."

45: "Karchah": Yarden notes that the animal was also referred to as a *tinna*, which is drawn from the Spanish word *tiña*—a disease that causes baldness. The creature's name recalls the Hebrew *keireyach*, or bald. Schirmann suggests that the name comes from the Greek *karcharias*—for "shark" (in Hebrew *karish*). *Baba Batra* 73–77 mentions a number of sea monsters and offers a variety of wild narratives and descriptions; 74a in particular mentions *karisa*, probably shark (see note to lines 71–72). Rosen-Moked notes that the name does not exist in related literatures or in contemporary books on zoology and sea-faring, or in dictionaries. She agrees with Schirmann and points out that a large shark could easily have upended the typical sailing vessels of the time, which were small.

46: Cf. Ezekiel 31:8.

49–50: Cf. Isaiah 33:21. Literally, "gallant ships" or "mighty craft."

56: Cf. Psalms 139:15.

57: Cf. Job 40:25: "Canst thou draw out Leviathan with a fish-hook?" Isaiah 27:1: "Leviathan the torturous serpent . . ."; Song of Songs 7:8: "And thy stature is like to a palm tree."

58: Cf. Isaiah 33:21: "But there the Lord will be with us in majesty, in a place of broad rivers and streams; wherein shall go no galley with oars."

60–62: Cf. Song of Songs 7:5: "Thy neck is as a tower of ivory; thine eyes as the pools in Heshbon" Song of Songs 4:15; Job 41:12: "Out of his nostrils goeth smoke"; Exodus 19:18: "And the smoke thereof ascended as the smoke of a furnace, and the whole mount [Sinai] quaked greatly"; Ezekiel 23:32; Job 40:23.

63–66: Cf. Psalms 119:83: "For I am become like a wine-skin in the smoke"; Judges 4:19; Ecclesiastes 10:12; Exodus 28:32: "And it shall have a hole for the head in the midst thereof; it shall have a binding of woven work around the hole of it, as it were the hole of a coat of mail. . ."; Exodus 39:23.

67–70: Cf. Song of Songs 7:3–5 (as above, lines 60–62); Psalms 91:4; Nahum 2:4: "The shield of his mighty men is made red."

71–72: Literally, "And its girth to those looking on was like Tyre in the midst of the sea or Dumah"—which refers to the two cities. The English plays off the word for Tyre (*Tsor*), akin to the Hebrew *tsur*, for cliff, rock, or fortress, or refuge. The modern city of Tyre is on a rocky peninsula that, during the time of Isaiah and Ezekiel, was an island. The biblical passage this verse is based on can be read in a number of ways. Cf. Ezekiel 27:32—old and new JPS versions:

"Who was there like Tyre fortified in the midst of the sea?" "Who was like Tyre when she was silenced in the midst of the sea?" Also, *Baba Batra* 73b: "Rabbah b. Bar Hana further stated: Once we were travelling on board a ship and saw a fish whose back was covered with sand out of which grew grass. Thinking it was dry land we went up and baked and cooked upon its back. When, however, its back was heated it turned, and had not the ship been nearby we should have been drowned."

73: Cf. Isaiah 10:14.

74–75: Cf. Job 40:17: "He straineth his tail like a cedar. . . ."

76–77: Cf. Ezekiel 21:12; Michah 1:4: "And the mountains shall be molten under Him, and the valleys shall be cleft, as wax before the fire, as waters that are poured down a steep place." Psalms 22:15: "I am poured out like water, and all my bones are out of joint; my heart is become like wax, it is melted in mine inmost parts"; Psalms 69:3: "and the flood overwhelms me."

78: Cf. Psalms 131:2: "Surely I have stilled and quieted my soul, like a weaned child with his mother"; Isaiah 53:7: "He was oppressed, though he humbled himself. . . . As a lamb that is led to the slaughter, And as a sheep that before her shearers is dumb."

82: Cf. 2 Kings 17:30. The Hebrew name Ashemah suggests "guilt" (*ashmah*).

83: Cf. Judges 18:4.

84: Cf. Proverbs 5:22: "His own iniquities shall ensnare the wicked."

85–86: Cf. Jonah 2:1–11.

87–88: Cf. Judges 9:16; Isaiah 3:10–11.

91–92: Cf. Exodus 15:1: "The horse and his rider hath He thrown into the sea"; Exodus 15:4: "And his chosen captains are sunk in the Red Sea."

94: Cf. 1 Samuel 25:37: "And his heart died within him and he became as a stone."

95: Cf. Zechariah 3:2: "The Lord rebuke thee, O Satan."

97–98: Cf. Psalms 22:7: "But I am a worm, and no man"; Job 25:6; Judges 9:48; Ezekiel 37:6: "And will bring up flesh upon you, and cover you with skin." This alludes to an Arabic saying—*dude al ude,* "a little worm on a branch."

100: Cf. Isaiah 9:16; Exodus 14:8: "For the children of Israel went out with a high hand."

108: Cf. Job 12:6: "And they that provoke God are secure."

109–112: Cf. Job 26:7: "He . . . hangeth the earth over nothing"; Psalms 95:5: "The sea is His, and He made it"; Isaiah 51:10.

112–114: Cf. Isaiah 44:10; Proverbs 8:23; Psalms 68:36.

115: Cf. *Berakhot* 54b: "Rab Judah said in the name of Rab: There are four [classes of people] who have to offer thanksgiving: those who have crossed the sea, those who have traversed the wilderness, one who has recovered from an illness, and a prisoner who has been set free. Whence do we know this of those who cross the sea? Because it is written, 'They that go down to the sea in ships, [that do business in great waters] . . . these saw the works of the Lord. . . . He raised the stormy wind . . . they mounted up to the heaven, they went down to the deeps. . . . they reeled to and fro and staggered like a drunken man. . . . they cried unto the Lord in their trouble, and He brought them out of their distresses. He made the storm a calm. . . . Let them give thanks unto the Lord for His mercy, and for His wonderful works to the children of men" (Psalms 107:23–31).

115–116: Cf. Deuteronomy 31:19: "Therefore write ye this song for you . . ."

117ff.: Cf. Isaiah 26:19; Daniel 12:2: "And many of them that sleep in the dust of the earth shall awake." The passage from here through to the end resembles Maimonides' Thirteen Articles of Faith (twelfth century) and several precursor-lists of "principles," beginning with Philo's eight principles: 1—the existence of God; 2—His unity; 3—divine Providence; 4—the creation of the world; 5—the unity of the world; 6—the existence of incorporeal ideas; 7—the revelation of the Law; and 8—its eternity (H. A. Wolfson, *Philo, Foundations of Religious Philosophy*). In the eleventh century, the North African sage Hananel b. Hushi'el declared four major beliefs: 1—in God; 2—in His eternity and unlikenes to any other being; 3—in the fact of His being the Creator of the world; and 4—in the advent of the Messiah. HaNagid's list is closest to Maimonides', which lists belief in the following: 1—The existence of God which is perfect and sufficient unto itself and which is the cause of all other beings; 2—God's unity which is unlike all other kinds of unity; 3—God cannot be conceived in bodily terms, and the anthropomorphic expressions applied to God in Scripture have to be understood in a metaphorical sense; 4—God is eternal; 5—God alone is to be worshiped and obeyed; 6—Prophecy; 7—Moses is unsurpassed by any other prophet; 8—The entire Torah was given to Moses; 9—Moses' Torah will not be abrogated or superseded by another divine law nor will anything be added to, or taken away from it; 10—God knows the actions of men; 11—God rewards those who fulfill the commandments of the Torah, and punishes those who transgress them; 12—the coming of the Messiah; and 13—the resurrection of the dead.

121–123: Cf. Ecclesiastes 12:10–11; *Baba Batra* 64a: "And I heard them say, 'Moses and his law are truth and we are liars'."

124–125: Cf. Proverbs 3:17.

126–128: Cf. Ecclesiastes 12:14: "For God shall bring every work into the judgment concerning every hidden thing"; Psalms 90:8: "Thou hast set our iniquities before Thee, our secret sins in the light of Thy countenance."

131: Cf. Exodus 20:17; Jeremiah 31:33: "I will put my Law in their inward parts, and in their heart will I write it."

A CURSE (218)

Lines 1–3: Literally, "My thoughts sling my heart like a sail-driven ship in a storm."

4–6: Literally, "And wandering is written in the book of God for my soul and roaming toward every state."

9: Literally, "move like Cain, and flee like Jonah." Cf. Genesis 4:12; Jonah 1:3.

THE APPLE (114, 116, 120, 121, 123, 124)

These six riddle-like poems are taken from the fifteen that HaNagid improvised and seem to be about the ornamental aesthetic of the Andalusian court. HaNagid was the most powerful Jew of his time, and, as the superscription indicates, he often hosted other courtiers and poets at his home for what in Arabic is called the *majlis* (session, council, or salon) where they would drink and talk and recite poems—many of which were accompanied by music. The superscription is a composite drawn from the original fifteen.

Line 5–8: This poem is the third in the series.

5: Cf. Song of Songs 4:14.

13–16: This poem is the seventh in the series. Cf. Psalms 104:15: "And wine that maketh glad the heart of man, making the face brighter than oil"; Proverbs 31:6–7: "Let him drink . . . and remember his misery no more"; *Eruvin* 65a: "R. Hanin observed: Wine was created for the sole purpose of comforting mourners and rewarding the wicked; for it is said, 'Give strong drink unto him that is ready to perish, and wine unto the bitter in soul.'"

17–20: This is the eighth poem in the series. Cf. Leviticus 8:8.

21–24: This poem is tenth in the series. Literally it reads: "Is there anything so astounding as the loudmouth in company whose tongue doesn't stick to the roof of his mouth? Or as the man who bites an apple and doesn't break his teeth on it or choke?" Cf. Ezekiel 35:13; Psalms 137:6; Lamentations 4:4.

25–27: This poem is the eleventh in the series. Cf. 2 Chronicles 13:5; Proverbs 22:10: "Cast out the scorner, and contention will go out."

JASMINE (129)

Line 2: Cf. Exodus 28:17.

THE GAZELLE (183)

The subject of homoeroticism in Hebrew poetry has generated a good deal of controversy, much of it amusing in its denial. Historically it simply is not clear just how that eroticism found expression in the Jewish community. What *is* clear is that—in distinction to the battle poems, for instance—the erotic poems do not necessarily reflect a biographical situation so much as they do a cultural reality.

In other words, while we do not know whether any of the Jewish poets had homosexual experience, we do know that Andalusian court culture was *not* homophobic, and that homoerotic poems were not uncommon. In any event the poems do not feel like the literary exercises some scholars make them out to be, and they might best be taken at face value, with all the ambiguity that implies.

Line 6: Cf. Deuteronomy 32:14: "And of the blood of the grape thou drankest foaming wine." A similar image is found in the Arabic poetry of Ibn Shuhaid (992–1035, Cordoba): "I kissed his throat, / a white jewel / drank the vivid red of his mouth / and so passed the night with him / deliciously until darkness smiled, / showing the white teeth of dawn." (trans. C. Franzen)

7: Literally, "cut like a *yod* [the tenth letter of the Hebrew alphabet—a crescent]." I have translated it as "D," for "Drink" and for the shape of the half moon as it curves to the right. The image of the moon like a letter is also common in Arabic poetry of the time, e.g.: "The air was clear, and the moon was bound in brightness, which shone toward the west, like a blue page with a silver dot, under a golden N."

THE FAWN (193)

Lines 7–8: The Hebrew has *bareket* for "pearl." Translations of the Bible usually render *bareket* as "emerald," "smaragd," or "agate"; the Gaonic period's understanding of the word implies a yellowish or whitish color. See Ibn Janakh, *Sepher HaShorashim*. Ibn Janakh was the first great Hebrew grammarian. His "dictionary" catalogued the roots of Hebrew, and he wrote extensively about Hebrew word formation. He was an Andalusian contemporary of HaNagid.

The image of the dark girl and the jewel is also found in Arabic poetry. The Spanish poet Ibn Khafaja (1058–1139) compares the star Sirius—the Dog Star, the hottest and brightest—burning in the darkness to a dinar (a coin) in a dark girl's palm.

WHERE'S THAT COY GAZELLE (160)

Line 1: Literally, "Where is that stammering [*illeg*] gazelle." Schirmann suggests that the line refers to the way in which the serving boys would make mistakes because of their foreign accents (perhaps on purpose, in order to tease the drinkers). In particular the sounds *r* and *g* gave them trouble. The terms "gazelle" and "fawn" are both taken from the Song of Songs, where they are masculine. Gazelle (*tsvi*) can also be feminine (*tsviyya*).

Reuben Tsur comments as follows: "In the garden parties of eleventh-century Moslem Spain, the feasting guests occasionally made love to the "gazelles," cupbearer boys, and poets wrote love poems to them. Some of these poems recorded a coquettish sweet-talk of these boys, with a regression to an infantile phonology. . . . /r/ is one of the child's latest acquisitions; indeed, an imperfect pronunciation of /r/ was prominent in the gazelle's speech. In Arabic and classical Hebrew /g/ has a fricative allophone closely resembling the guttural /R/; it is this velar fricative /gh/ that the gazelle substitutes for the /r/. . .'" Cf. Abu Nuwas: "My heart melts on account of the gazelle, I desire him / the effect of the r in his mouth, as he articulates it" (trans. R. Tsur).

The term *illeg* is from Isaiah 32:4—"the tongue of the stammerers shall be ready to speak plainly" (old JPS version); or "And the tongues of mumblers shall speak with fluent elegance" (new JPS). Rashi, commenting on that verse, explains the term as follows: "Anyone who doesn't know how to compose his speech to be elegant is called *illeg* . . ." Moshe Ibn Ezra uses an Arabic word from the same root (i-l-g) in his *Book of Remembrance and Discussion*: "And our language calls those who are not well-spoken (*illegim*)."

2: Cf. Song of Songs 6:2.
3: Cf. Song of Songs 3:6; Exodus 30:23.
6: Literally, "covered."
7: Cf. Proverbs 25:15: "And a soft tongue breaketh the bone. . . "
8: Cf. Exodus 4:11.
9: Cf. Jeremiah 8:7: "The stork in the heaven knoweth her appointed times; and the turtle and the swallow and the crane."
10: Literally, "He wanted to say *ra* (bad) and said to me *ga* (touch)."
11: Cf. 2 Samuel 1:16: "thy mouth hath testified against thee."
13: Literally, "He wished to say *surah* (leave) but said *sugah* (set about, as in the line from the Song of Songs, "Thy belly is like a heap of wheat, set about by roses."). Cf. Song of Songs 7:3. The English here tries to reflect the sort of linguistic slippage that a non-native speaker experiences.

IN FACT I LOVE THAT FAWN (162)

Lines 1–2: Cf. Song of Songs 6:2: "My beloved is gone down to his garden, to the beds of spices, to feed in the gardens, and to gather lilies." (The words for "lily" and "rose" are often confused.)
2: Literally, "who is picking roses in your garden."
3: Cf. Exodus 15:7.
4–5: Literally, "If you could see the one I love with your eyes / your lovers would pursue you but you would not be there." Cf. Job 7:21: "For now shall I lie down in the dust; and Thou wilt seek me but I shall not be."
6–7: Cf. Judges 14:9: "But he told them not that he had scraped the honey out of the body of the lion."
11: Cf. Joshua 3:10: "Hereby ye shall know that the living God is among you."

12: Cf. 1 Samuel 25:24: "And she fell at his feet, and said: 'Upon me, my lord, upon me be the iniquity.'"

I'LL SHOW YOU A FAWN (171)

Lines 1–3: Literally, "hurt your heart" or "put sorrow in your heart." Cf. Leviticus 26:16: "I will appoint a terror over you, even consumption and fever, that shall make the eyes to fail, and the soul to languish. . ."
4: Literally, "Blessed be He . . . "
7: Cf. Genesis 49:3.
9–10: Cf. Deuteronomy 32:30: "How should one chase a thousand, And two put ten thousand to flight?"
    Cf. the Andalusian Arabic poet Ash-Sharif at-Taliq (961–1009): "He charms us with the intensely white and black eyes of a white antelope whose glance is an arrow notched [to be aimed] at my heart." (Trans. J. Monroe)

THEY STOLE MY SLEEP (178)

Line 4: Cf. 1 Kings 3:26: "It shall be neither mine nor thine; divide it." This is the story of King Solomon and the child.

HIS BROTHER'S ILLNESS (86)

Lines 1–2: Literally, "My limbs [or bones] filled with pangs [or pain] and grief." Cf. Genesis 2:23; 1 Samuel 4:19; Isaiah 21:3.
3–4: Literally, "And my eyes pour out without ceasing." Cf. Lamentations 3:49.
15–18: Cf. Job 19:4: "And be it indeed that I have erred, mine error remaineth with myself." Literally, "the errors will remain within me."

ON THE DEATH OF ISAAC, HIS BROTHER
(87–95, 100–101, 103–4)

The poems included under this title are taken from a series of 18 poems that HaNagid composed in the wake of his brother Isaac's death. Each is accompanied by a superscription. In order not to break the flow of the series, I have noted below the superscriptions for all but the first poem in the series. The order of the poems in some cases departs from that of the diwan.

I rushed (87): Line 3, literally, "crushed and lowered." Cf. Psalms 9:10.
5: Literally, "I said to him, 'Tell me, why are you silent? Is Isaac alive?'"

7–8: Literally, "And I responded. . ." Cf. *Baba Batra* 16a: "Rab said: Dust should be put in the mouth of Job, because he makes himself the colleague of heaven. . . . Dust should be placed in the mouth of Job: is there a servant who argues with his master?"

9: Literally, "May you hear of all trouble and distress." Cf. Proverbs 1:27.

13–14: Literally, "How could one die who was great in his generation and prized by most of his brothers and a seeker of good for your people?" Cf. Esther 10:3: "For Mordechai the Jew . . . was great among the Jews, and accepted of the multitude of his brethren; seeking the good of his people, and speaking peace to all his seed."

18: Literally, "whether prince or pauper?" Cf. Leviticus 25:47.

First child of my mother (91): Superscription: "And he recited this in which he describes his going in to see him and his kissing him while he was lying on his bed."

Line 1: Literally, "Firstborn of my mother, the first of death [the angel of death] has stolen you." The English has departed somewhat to maintain, at least rhythmically, a semblance of the Hebrew's weave and the tension between "firstborn" and "first of death." Cf. Job 18:13: "Yea, the first-born of death shall devour his members."

9: Literally, "curtain."

12: Literally, "on the day of your affliction [or misfortune]."

13: Cf. *Eruvin* 65b: "R. Ila'i said: By three things may a person's character be determined: By his cup (*koso*), by his purse (*keeso*), and by his anger (*ka'aso*)." Also Psalms 16:5.

22–27: Cf. Isaiah 29:10: "For the Lord hath poured out upon you the spirit of deep sleep, and hath closed your eyes."

28–30: Literally, "They gave you to drink in ripeness of age from the cup of death, and soon I'll drink from your cup." Cf. Job 5:26, 30:2; and *Bereshit Rabbah* 79:1: "And you will come fresh toward the grave."

31: HaNagid was 48 at the time.

Why should I force (89): Superscription: "And he said when he tore his clothes in mourning for him:"

Line 1–4: Literally, "Why should I tear my clothes and garments [as a traditional sign of mourning]?" Cf. 1 Samuel 4:12; Job 13:28: "Though I am . . . like a garment that is moth-eaten"; Joel 2:13: "And rend your heart and not your garments." See note to line 13.

5–8: Literally, "Why put dirt on my robes [or dress]?"—which was a traditional sign of mourning. The "slime-filled pits" HaNagid refers to allude to the biblical Vale of Siddim, which was filled with slime pits, or pits of bitumen. Cf. Genesis 14:10: "Now the vale of Siddim was full of slime pits, and the kings of Sodom and Gomorrah fled, and they fell there."

11–12: Breaking cups was another sign of mourning.

13–16: The Hebrew plays on the words for "walls" or "sides" of my heart (*tseedei levavi*) and "thorns" (*tsiddim*). The melic weave also contains additional elements that are too complicated to trace here (for example, see line 8, *"siddim"*). Again I have tried to set up acoustic correspondences in place of the puns. Cf. Judges 2:3; and *Mo'ed Katan* 22b: "For all [other—except for one's father and mother] dead, one tacks the rent together after seven [days] and [completely] reunites [the edges] after thirty [days]. . ."

17–18: Literally, "the walls of my heart. . ." Cf. Jeremiah 4:19: "Oh, the walls of my heart! My heart moans within me."

19–20: In other words, the pain will continue well after the official display of mourning is over. Cf. Ecclesiastes 9:8.

21–24: Cf. Exodus 25:15: "The staves shall be in the rings of the [holy] ark; they shall not be taken from it."

27–28: Literally, "from my soul [my life] will forever be distant."

My language (92): Superscription: "And he said in description of his being wrapped in the shroud and lowered into his grave, may God have mercy upon him:"

Line 1: Literally, "My tongue [or language]." The Hebrew carries the double meaning that the contemporary English "tongue" strains for. Cf. Judges 8:24.

6–7: The Hebrew here means that Isaac was like a father to HaNagid and others. He was a friend who looked out for them.

9: Cf. Hosea 5:11: "Ephraim is defrauded, robbed of redress." [Hebrew uncertain.]

10–12: Cf. Job 31:32: "my doors I opened to the roadside."

13–15: Cf. Psalms 78:72; Isaiah 11:7–9: "And the cow and the bear shall feed; their young ones shall lie down together."

19: Cf. Jeremiah 4:31: "For I have heard a voice as of a woman in travail, the anguish as of her that bringeth forth her first child."

21–22: Cf. 1 Samuel 4:12. See note to "Why Should I Force," lines 1 and 13. Cf. *Mo'ed Katan* 22b and 24a: "For all [other] dead, if he desires, he bares [his shoulder—and also bares his heart] and if he does not desire he does not bare it. . ." "Samuel said, 'Any rending [of clothes] not done in the flush [of grief] is not a [proper] rending. . .'" A line of the original has been omitted here: "my face covered."

28–29: Cf. 2 Samuel 19:1: "Thus [King David] said: 'O my son Absolom . . . would I had died for thee."

36: "My soul" is a literal reading. The expression often means "my life." Cf. Psalms 22:20: "O Thou my strength . . ."; 1 Kings 19:4: "O Lord, Take away my life, for I am not better than my fathers."

And I returned (94): Superscription: "He visited his grave on the second day after the burial and said:"

Line 1–2: Cf. Job 7:11: "I will speak in the anguish of my spirit." Also, *Semahot* VIII: "We go out to the cemetery and examine the dead within three days and do not fear [being suspected of] superstitious practices."

3–4: Cf. Genesis 43:29: "And he [Joseph] lifted up his eyes, and saw Bejamin his brother . . . and said, 'God be gracious unto thee. . .'"

7: Cf. Job 23:2: "Even today is my complaint bitter."

9–10: Literally, "Can't you hear me. . ."

15–16: Literally, "Is the place of your jaw hollowed out," which involves a play on Judges 15:19: "But God hath cleaved the hollow-place-in-the-jaw-bone" (a place name, "the hollow place at Lehi [jaw]").

17–19: Literally, "Has your vigor abated?" Cf. Deuteronomy 34:7. This is the phrase used to describe Moses at the end of his life.

22: Literally, "Who has taken me [from the womb]."

23–25: "My promise" here is both an epithet for God (Cf. Psalms 22:10) and refers to HaNagid's work on earth and with his "tongue," as in his vow in poem 92. Cf. Isaiah 57:1–2.

Tell him, please (95): Superscription: "And afterward he said:"

Line 4: Cf. Proverbs 27:20: "The "netherworld and destruction are never satiated." "Destruction" in the Hebrew plays on the root for "lost."

10: Literally, "Until I'm laid by his side." The repetition of "dust" mirrors the repetition of the *esh* sound in the Hebrew, which runs through the poem and, on its own, means "fire."

Could condolence persuade me? (93): Superscription: "And he said about the condolences that he received from others":

Line 1: Literally, "Could you speak to my heart with condolences?"

3: Literally, "How can I have knowledge [or discernment] after Isaac?"

5: Literally, "Leave off me and don't multiply words." Cf. Isaiah 22:4.

6–8: Literally, "Leave me and stand away from [or opposite] me."

9: Literally, "Hurry and entreat me to the jackal who mourns. . ." Cf. Isaiah 22:4; Genesis 23:8; Micah 1:8: "I will make a wailing like the jackals"; Job 30:29: "I am become a brother to jackals."

12: Literally, "and see who overcomes [whom] in bitterness."

13–14: Cf. Lamentations 2:13: "What shall I liken to thee, O daughter of Jerusalem? What shall I equal to thee that I may comfort thee? . . . For thy breach is great like the sea."

Give up, heart (88): Superscription: "And then he said:"

Line 1: Cf. Ecclesiastes 2:20.

5–8: Literally, "Live after him in misery, and if you'd request respite from his grief [the grief of his death], die like him."

When the name Isaac is called out across me (90): This translation is composed of excerpts from a longer poem which begins: *"Yemahair yom pekudatee"* ("May the day of my judgment come quickly.") The superscription reads: "And he poured forth this elegy, the longest of all the elegies he composed for him, and in it mentioned three of his family who died after him." The English picks up on line 22 of the Yarden edition.

Line 2: Literally, "my soul grows hot." Cf. Psalms 39:4; Deuteronomy 19:6; Job 16:13.

4: Cf. Psalms 126:2: "Then was our mouth filled with laughter, and our tongue was singing." Lamentations 1:7.

6–7: Literally, "And I hold back like Joseph. . ." "Act the horizon" plays on the root for "to hold back" (*et-a-p-ek*) and horizon (*o-ph-ek*). Cf. Genesis 43:30–31: "And he refrained himself . . . [from weeping]."

10: A line from the Hebrew is omitted here: "And I went down into the deep pit and laid him, and I went out. . ."

11: Or, "like my life."

12: Literally, "as though he hadn't lain as a youth by my side in my bed."

13: Literally, "or not sat at school and religious study with me in my youth."

15: Cf. Job 7:5. Five lines in the Hebrew are skipped here.

16: Cf. Jeremiah 16:19: "O Lord, my strength and my stronghold, and my refuge."

18–19: The English now returns to the beginning of the Hebrew, line 2.

20: The English moves to lines 12–17 of the original.

23–27: Cf. Psalms 69:22: "They put poison into my food, and in my thirst they gave me vinegar to drink"; Job 20:14: "Yet his food in his bowels [stomach] is turned, it is the gall of asps within him"; Deuteronomy 32:33; Job 20:16.

27: Literally, "and my tears and the blood of my eyes mix with drink."

28: The English moves to line 42 of the Hebrew. Cf. Proverbs 15:30.

31–35: HaNagid here refers to the fact that three other family members have died since Isaac was buried. The English adds "What of the others?"

34: Literally, "And did you take three from my house and my culture and lay them around you. . . ?"

36: The English moves to line 52 of the Hebrew. Cf. Psalms 132:4: "I will not give sleep to mine eyes, nor slumber to mine eyelids."

38: A line of the Hebrew is omitted here: "And understand that tomorrow my being crushed will come."

39: "And understand that. . . ."

40: Cf. Ecclesiastes 2:14–16: "As it happeneth to the fool, so will it happen even to me, and why was I then more wise?"

A brother is in me (101): Superscription: "And he recited this when his letters stopped and others' arrived instead:"

Line 3–4: Cf. Jeremiah 2:25.

Twelve months have passed (103): Superscription: "And he recited this after a year had passed since his death:"

Line 2–3: Cf. Psalms 91:3: "He will deliver thee from the snare of the fowler, and from the noisome pestilence."

4: Cf. Job 21:33: "The clods of the valley are sweet unto him."

7: Cf. Psalms 107:32.

9–10: Cf. Zechariah 14:12: "Their flesh shall consume away . . . and their eyes shall consume away in their sockets."

11: Cf. Ezekiel 37:11: "Our bones are dried up"; Isaiah 56:3: "Behold, I am a dry tree."

13–14: Literally, "eats along his skin." Cf. Isaiah 50:9: "They all shall wax old as a garment, the moth shall eat them up."

Time, which betrays us (100): Superscription: "And his sorrow for him was great at the end of a year since his death and he recited the following:"

Line 1: Literally, "Traitor time."

2–5: A number of allusive adverbial phrases in the Hebrew translate awkwardly, so I have added several phrases in the English to mirror their effect. Cf. Deuteronomy 34:7.

9–10: Cf. Jeremiah 22:10: "Weep sore for him that goeth away, for he shall return no more"; Psalms 78:39.

11–13: Literally, "I acquired with your death heart and cleverness [or cunning] and during your life I was deceived." Cf. Proverbs 15:32, 19:8.

14: Literally, "I thought you would live for [with] me forever and ever, but time thought otherwise." Cf. Isaiah 10:7.

A psalm for the hearer (104): Superscription: "And when his grief had passed and he was consoled in his mourning he recited the following:" This poem is also found in *Ben Kohelet* (poem 395, Abramson), with several variants.

Lines 1–2: Cf. Psalms 65:3: "O Thou that hearest prayer, to Thee doth all flesh come."

3: Cf. Psalms 33:1.

5: Cf. Psalms 49:3.

7–13: Literally, "because all which is great and hard, he created soft and young in the beginning." Yarden notes the parallel in the Arabic poetry of Abu ali Al-qali al-Baghdadi: "God, may He be magnified and exalted, created everything small, and after a time they grow large, except for grief, which he created large and which becomes smaller with time."

9: "Labor": the Hebrew word might also be translated as "creation" or "production."

11: Cf. Hosea 4:13; Isaiah 6:13.

14–16: Literally, "And if grief remains in a heart as at the outset. . . ."

17: Literally, "From *elohim* (God)."

22: Cf. Numbers 22:24: "like a lane between the vineyard." This alludes to Balaam, who is about to have his foot crushed against the wall of the "lane."

24: Literally, "And my worry runs out. . ."

27: Cf. Ezekiel 1:24: "a noise of tumult, like the noise of a host."

31–32: Cf. Job 5:18.

33–35: Literally, "May He who wraps [swaddles] the darkness [or mist], and wraps my mother's eldest with dirt, forgive his transgressions. . ." Cf. Job 33:9.

37–39: Literally, "And with the fathers who were righteous and his treasure, may he be counted as treasure." Cf. Exodus 19:5; Ecclesiastes 2:8: "I gathered me also silver and gold and treasure. . ." Also Ibn Janakh, under "S-g-l."

HaNagid was plagued throughout his career by enemies who could not tolerate the prominence of a Jew in a Moslem government. Various alliances were formed against him, though none were successful. This poem of friendship alludes to the conspiracies. Epistolary verse figured prominently in the diwans of the Andalusian courtier poets, and "poems of friendship" (for and against it) were frequently exchanged. The majority of these were overwhelmingly conventional, but there are strong poems of direct address in the group as well.

Line 1–2: Cf. Song of Songs 8:9.

7: Cf. *Hullin* 61a: "The turtle dove has an extra toe and a crop. . ."

11–12: Cf. Proverbs 1:17: "In vain the net is spread." *Pesachim* 3: "A certain Syrian [i.e. non-Jew] used to go up and partake of the Passover sacrifices in Jerusalem, boasting: It is written, 'there shall no alien eat thereof . . . no uncircumcised person shall eat thereof' [Exodus 12:43, 48], yet I eat of the very best. Said R. Judah b. Bathyra to him: Did they supply you with the fat-tail? No, he replied. [Then] when you journey up thither say to them, Supply me with the fat-tail. When he went up he said to them, Supply me with the fat-tail. But the fat-tail belongs to the Most High! they replied. [It is burned on the altar and 'goes up']. Who told you [to do] this? they enquired. R. Judah b. Bathyra, answered he. What is this [matter] before us? they wondered. They investigated his pedigree, and discovered that he was a Syrian, and killed him. ['For a non-Jew might not even penetrate beyond a certain point within the temple precints on pain of death, and a public notice gave due warning of this.' Josephus *Antiquities* XV, 11:5.] Then they sent [a message] to R. Judah b. Bathyra: 'Peace be with thee, R. Judah b. Bathyra, for thou art in Nisibis yet thy net is spread in Jerusalem.'" Cf. *Avot* 3:16: "He would say . . . 'And a net is cast over all the living . . . And the judgment is a true judgment, and everything is ready for the meal.'"

18–19: Cf. *Ketubot* 52b: "A father must provide for his daughter clothes and covering and must also give her a dowry so that people may be anxious to woo her and . . . marry her. And to what extent? Both Abaye and Raba ruled: Up to a tenth of his wealth." Also: Deuteronomy 21:17.

23–25: Cf. Proverbs 10:18: "He that uttereth a slander is a fool."

26–27: Cf. Psalms 22:8: "All they that see me laugh me to scorn; they shoot out the lip, they shake the head."

29–31: Cf. Job 15:34–35; Isaiah 54:1.

35: Cf. Deuteronomy 34:7.

39: In his introduction to *Sepher Hilkhot haNagid* Mordechai Margolioth states that "HaNagid was the greatest Talmudist of his generation in Spain . . ." Except for the fragments of *Hilkheta Gavrata*, which Margolioth has edited, all of HaNagid's halakhic writings have been lost. (This is also the case with his philological work and his other religious writing.) The well-known introduction to the Talmud by Shmuel HaNagid is actually by Shmuel ben Hofni Gaon of Egypt, not ibn Nagrela.

THE HOUSE OF PRAYER (83)

Yarden classifies this as a "poem of wit."

Line 1: Literally, "Has time become insolent on Rabbi [Judah HaNasi, the redactor of the Mishnah in the third century CE] and Rava [a Babylonian Amora, or teacher who died in 352 CE]." Cf. Isaiah 3:5: "The child shall behave insolently against the aged, and the base against the honorable."

5–6: Mephibosheth was Saul's grandson and Jonathan's son. Tsiba was Saul's servant. Cf. 2 Samuel 9:6–13. Also *Berakhot* 4a: "Why then was he called Mephibosheth? Because he humiliated David in the Halachah." (*Me-phi-bosheth* means "Out of my mouth humiliation.")

6: Rav Hai HaGaon was the last of the Babylonian *Gaonim*, or leaders of the Yeshivot there. The leading Talmudist of HaNagid's time, he died in 1038.

7: Cf. Numbers 15:38: "And bid them that they make them . . . fringes in the corners of their garments."

10: The allusion is to the holiday of Hoshana Rabba, on the seventh day of Sukkot, when willow sprigs are beaten in the synagogue. Margolioth's *Sepher Hilkhot haNagid* contains the following entry (14): "And Rabbi Shmuel Halevi said it is still a point of controversy, some circle with the lulav and some circle with the willow. . ." (p. 113). Margolioth comments: "HaNagid is alluding to the controversy between [the halakha of] Babylonia and [the halakha of] Eretz Yisrael. Apparently the Eretz Yisraeli or Palestinian practice of circling the altar with willow branches on Hoshana Rabba was brought to Spain in the generation preceeding HaNagid and perhaps HaNagid took it from his teacher R. Hanokh, who brought the practice from Bari, which is in Italy."

11: HaNagid is referring to the sound of a crowd one often hears coming from a synagogue or house of study. Cf. *Berakhot* 3a: "In the first watch, the ass brays."

17–19: Genesis 37:30: "And as for me, whither shall I go"; Isaiah 8:20. Literally, "They've changed the testimony and Torah . . ."

22: Literally, "like a tamarisk in the wilderness." The students were moving their bodies as is traditional during study and prayer. Cf. Jeremiah 17:6.

23: "The great": Literally, "In their mouths they abused Hillel and Shammai / and struck on the cheek Rabbi Akiva." Cf. 2 Kings 19:22; Micah 4:14. Hillel and Shamai are the two major authorities cited in the Mishnah. Akiva is one of the great heroes of post-biblical Judaism. One of the most important *tannaim*, or scholars of the first generation, he died while being tortured by the Romans during the Bar Kohba Rebellion, circa 132 CE.

25: The teacher would take whatever noise they made as a sign of comprehension and agreement and go on with his nonsense.

30–31: Cf. Daniel 10:6: "like the voice of a multitude." *Menachot* 43b: "R. Meir used to say, A man is bound to say one hundred blessings daily, as it is written, "And now, Israel, what doth the Lord thy God require of thee? [The Hebrew word for 'what' (*ma*) is interpreted as though it were *me'ah*, which means 'a hundred.']"

32–33: Cf. *Menachot* 43b: "R. Judah used to say, A man is bound to say the following three blessings daily: '[Blessed art thou . . .] who hast not made me a heathen,' '. . . who hast not made me a woman'; and . . . 'who hast not made me a brutish man.'" The prayer 'who hast not made me a woman' is part of the morning liturgy.

34–35: Literally, "Would you put your soul among the males [or masculine], when the Lord will testify against you that you are feminine?" The word for 'feminine' (*nekevah*) is akin to the words for 'punctured' or 'holed' (*nakuv*), 'anus' (*nakuva*), and 'to blaspheme' (*nakav*).

THE CRITIQUE (82)

Likewise a poem of wit according to Yarden.

Line 1: Cf. Psalms 45:14: "All glorious is the king's daughter within the palace, her raiment is of chequer work wrought with gold."

2: Cf. Ecclesiastes 2:8. The Hebrew here involves a hapaxlegomenon, a word which appears only once in the Bible. Some versions—the old JPS—interpret the word to mean "pretty woman" or "mistress" and translate the phrase from Ecclesiastes as "women very many" or "and many concubines" (Revised Version). The King James version has "music instruments." Others—the new JPS version—adopt the Mishnaic usage of the word and translate "coffers and coffers of them [of luxuries]." Yarden reads "fountain."

3: Cf. Isaiah 10:16: "a burning like the burning of fire . . ."

4: Cf. Psalms 45:9; Exodus 30:23–24: "the chief spices . . . flowing myrrh . . . sweet calamus . . . and cassia."

8: Literally, "while yours were white (as hail)."

9–10: Cf. Numbers 31:23: "it shall be purified with the water of sprinkling." Literally, "but this poem is impure."

11: A line from the Hebrew has been omitted here. Literally, "I weighed it against your poems, which were as grooms, but this one among them would be outlawed." Cf. Jeremiah 31:20.

16: Cf. Psalms 57:5: "and their tongue a sharp sword."

THE PAIN (80)

Another poem of wit according to Yarden.

Line 6–7: Literally, "there's no hope that he'll get up [and leave]."
9–12: Literally, "What can I do, since Sisera has come and there is no Yael from the House of Hever. Come quickly and do for him as Abraham did for Shemever [ally of Sodom]." In other words, "Save me as you saved Shemever." I have reworked the line from the same story for sound and to make the allusion more accessible. Sisera was a Canaanite military leader who was eventually slain by the Israelite woman Yael, who tricked Sisera and then drove a spike through his forehead. Chedorlaomer was the king of Elam and, in the time of Abraham, went to war against Sodom and enslaved its population, including Lot, Abraham's nephew. Abraham pursued Chedorlaomer, defeated his forces, and rescued Lot. Cf. Judges 4:17–21, Genesis 14.

WHAT ARE THESE (113)

This poem is catalogued in the Yarden edition under "Poems of Entertainment," along with the apple poems. It, too, is a riddle.

A DAY OF DISTRESS (1)

This battle poem is the first poem in the Yarden edition. There are forty-one battle poems in all. While HaNagid wrote few liturgical poems per se, he often wove religious elements including prayer into his martial verse.

The superscription to another pre-battle poem that uses the same imagery of distress, fire, and water (3 in Yarden) states explicitly that the poem took the place of afternoon prayers on that day.

Line 1: Cf. Zephaniah 1:15: "a day of trouble and distress . . . of darkness and gloominess." Psalms 119:143: "Trouble and anguish have overtaken me, yet thy commandments are my delight"; Psalms 102:3: "Hide not Thy face from me in the day of my distress."
2: Cf. 2 Samuel 18:27.
3–4: Cf. Psalms 119:68: "Thou art good, and doest good." *Baba Metzia* 49a: "Abaye said: That means that one must not speak one thing with the mouth and another with the heart."
7: Cf. 2 Samuel 22:2–3; Psalms 18:3, 69:30.
11: Micha'el—One of the three archangels. According to the *Sepher Bahir* 11, he is the "The prince of water and hail."

12: Cf. Isaiah 43:1: "Thus saith the Lord"; Proverbs 22:23: "For the Lord will plead their cause"; Judges 6:31: "He will contend for him."

13–15: Cf. Isaiah 43:2: "When thou passest through the waters, I will be with thee, and through the rivers, they shall not overflow thee"; Psalms 27:2: "When evil-doers came upon me."

16: Cf. *Pesachim* 118a: "Said Gabriel. . . . 'But I, the Prince of fire . . .'" Also *Sepher Bahir,* 11.

19–20: Cf. Isaiah 43:2: "When thou walkest through the fire, thou shalt not be burned, neither shall the flame kindle upon thee."

THE VICTORY OVER SEVILLE (4)

This poem chronicles events surrounding HaNagid's battle with Ben Abbad, the commander of the army of Seville, which is approximately 140 miles west of Granada. Seville was the largest and most powerful of the Taifa states. Ashtor estimates that its population was in the area of 90,000 residents (others say 55,000 is more realistic), 6% of which were Jews. Granada had fewer than a third of that number and was known as the "city of the Jews."

The poem is essentially a "victory poem," and HaNagid calls it "Tehilla," a psalm (after Psalm 145). The Hebrew has 149 lines to it, for the number of biblical Psalms recognized in HaNagid's time. Schirmann notes that this was HaNagid's second large battle and still involved a new experience for him. Subsequent battle poems are shorter, usually by half.

Line 5–8: Cf. Isaiah 43:2; see also "A Day of Distress," note to lines 13 and 19, and Exodus 15:8.

9: Cf. Psalms 33:1: "Praise is comely for the upright."

12: Cf. Isaiah 1:25: "I will purge away thy dross as with lye, and take away all thine alloy"; Proverbs 6:34.

16: Cf. Deuteronomy 22:12.

17–18: Cf. Isaiah 43:3; Job 21:30.

19: HaNagid is referring to the battle at Alfuente in 1038, about which he composed another 149-line (in the Hebrew) poem. During that battle HaNagid had defeated Ben Abbas, the vizier to Zuhair, King of Almeria, a coastal city some 80 miles southeast of Granada. According to Dozy, Ben Abbas too was known for his exceptional epistolary talent. And he too wrote verses, though these were more amateurish than those of his Jewish counterpart and were mocked by his peers. Ben Abbas was extremely vain and wealthy. As "an Arab of pure blood," he hated the Berbers and the Jews, and wanted to avoid an alliance with the Granadans at all costs. He launched a slander campaign against HaNagid, hoping to have him dismissed from his post, and when that did not work he persuaded his Slavic king, Zuhair, to aid one of Granada's many rivals. When war eventually broke out between Almeria and Granada on August 3, 1038, Zuhair's forces under Ben Abbas were defeated near the village of Alfuente, which lay in the mountainous countryside near Granada. Zuhair was killed while fighting, and Ben Abbas was taken prisoner and eventually executed. HaNagid's poem declares the day of victory a Purim of its own, and sent word of the victory to the Jews of Africa, Egypt, Eretz Yisrael, and Babylonia.

21: Ben Abbad was the son of Seville's ruler, the Khadi, or judge. Ben Abbas was not of royal lineage. Cf. Jeremiah 13:21; Esther 6:8.

30: Cf. Job 29:23: "And they waited for me as for the rain."

31: Badis was HaNagid's king.

33: Both Badis and Ben Abbad.

37–38: Cf. Ezekiel 28:9; Jeremiah 51:40: "I will bring them down like rams to the slaughter"; Exodus 15:11.

39–40: Cf. Leviticus 5:15; Judges 18:7.

43: Cf. He had taken Carmona, a Berber kingdom (city) approximately 20 miles east of Seville. Ibn Burzal, king of Carmona, had previously been an ally of the Khadi; but when he was attacked, Ibn Burzal turned to Badis of Granada and Idris of Malaga, who had been his enemies up until then.

44: A few words of the original have been omitted, literally, "There was no one to stop it."

50–51: Cf. 2 Samuel 3:34; Deuteronomy 17:5.

52: Cf. Psalms 83:4

53: The Hebrew can mean either "set them in shackles" or "took the shoes from their feet." Cf. Psalm 60:10; Ruth 4:7.

54–55: Cf. 2 Samuel 20:19: "Seekest thou to destroy a city and a mother in Israel? Why wilt thou swallow up the inheritance of the Lord?"

57: Cf. Deuteronomy 8:14.

58: Cf. Job 17:2.

61: Al Mu'tamid of Seville (1040–1095) wrote: "Warriors like lions live there. . ."

62: Cf. Judges 7:12: "like locusts for a multitude."

64: Cf. Leviticus 3:4: "And the two kidneys, and the fat that is on them, which is by the loins."

65: Cf. 2 Kings 3:21: "all that were able to put on armor."

68: Cf. Deuteronomy 28:47.

69–70: Cf. 1 Samuel 17:5; Nahum 2:4: "the shield of his mighty men is made red." Literally, "red as parchment." Yarden notes that deer parchment is red.

71: Cf. Isaiah 60:8; Psalms 55:9.

72: Cf. 1 Samuel 17:5–7: "and he had greaves of brass upon his legs and a javelin of brass between his shoulders, and the shaft of his spear . . ."

75: Cf. Genesis 3:24.

77: According to Schirmann, HaNagid has distorted the progress of the battle. Schirmann notes that both Badis and Ibn Bakanna (head of the Malagan army) retreated when they saw the size of Ben Abbad's army. Ben Abbad then chased after Badis and would have routed his army had not Badis's call for help gotten out to Ibn Bakanna. The two armies rejoined forces and surprised Ben Abbad's troops at Ecija.

80: Cf. Isaiah 1:22: "Thy silver is become dross, thy wine mixed with water."

81: Cf. Jeremiah 23:32; 1 Kings 22:20–22.

83: Cf. Isaiah 19:3.

89: Cf. Deuteronomy 25:18.

92: The English omits a phrase that refers to "the day of the river valleys," when God appeared to help the Israelites. Cf. Numbers 21:25 and the Targum Yerushalmi: "When the children of Israel crossed the River Arnon the Moabites hid in the caves by the river, saying: when the children of Israel cross we will come out against them and kill them and the Lord of the world . . . signaled to the mountains and they leaned their heads toward one another and crushed the warriors' heads and the rivers ran with the blood of the slain." The battle with Ben Abbad took place at the River Genil, which runs between Granada and Ecija, the latter being approximately 50 miles east of Seville.

93: Cf. Proverbs 30:27.

94: Cf. Exodus 32:18; Jeremiah 2:15, 48:36: "my heart moaneth like pipes."

96: Agag—Zuhair, the king of Almeria, whom HaNagid had fought the previous year during the battle at Alfuente. Cf. Esther 3:1.

98: Cf. Isaiah 19:16: "In that day shall Egypt be like unto women; and it shall tremble in fear."

101–102: Cf. Esther 6:8; Ezekiel 27:24.

106: Amalekites refers to the Slavs, the army of Zuhair, whom HaNagid's forces defeated at Alfuente. Cf. Exodus 17:8–14.

107–108: Cf. Job 32:6: "Therefore I was too awestruck and fearful . . ." (NJPS). "The children of might" refers to the army of Granada, which HaNagid commanded.

112: Cf. Ezekiel 16:30.

113–114: Joel 4:2; Proverbs 16:33.

115: Literally, "the first born of death," which is the traditional epithet for the angel of death. Cf. Job 18:13.

118: Literally, "in the chorus of seventy banners," which refers to the host of angels surrounding the throne of God. Each represented one of the nations of the world. Cf. *Pirke de Rabbi Eleazar* 24: "The Lord called to the seventy angels surrounding his throne and said to them: 'Come—we'll confound their speech,' and the Lord went down with the seventy angels and counfounded the speech of the nations and the seventy tongues and appointed an angel over each nation."

Also—*Song of Songs Rabbah* 2:4: "He brought me down to the house of wine . . . to the great wine cellar, this is Sinai, and there I saw Micha'el and his banner and Gabriel and his banner. . ."

120: Yarden refers to Sa'adia Gaon's saying that "The ancients knew the name of the Lord [the correct pronunciation of the tetragrammaton] the mighty founders of the earth would invoke whenever necessary in times of trouble and distress."

121: Literally, "to overcome enemy forces. . ." The English tries to account for the weave in the Hebrew: "*L'hitgabair alai chail tsar b'chail tsur.*"

122: Cf. 1 Kings 20:1.

128: Cf. *Talmud Yerushalmi, Berakhot* 2:5a: "That He would prevent wantonness from coming into the world."

130: Cf. Psalms 16:6, ASV: "The lines have fallen to me in pleasant places." NJPS: "Delightful country has fallen to my lot."

131: Cf. Psalms 58:7: "Break out the cheek-teeth of the young lions"; Job 4:10: "the teeth of the young lions are broken."

133: Cf. Isaiah 59:17: "And he put on garments of vengeance . . . and was clad with zeal as a cloak."

134: Cf. Ezekiel 30:9; Exodus 15:10.

136–137: Cf. Song of Songs 2:9: "He looketh in through the windows, he peereth through the lattice. . . "

138–140: Cf. Hosea 13:3: "as the chaff that is driven with the wind out of the threshing-floor"; Isaiah 64:5.

142–143: Cf. Psalms 29:6: "He maketh them also to skip like a calf, Lebanon and Sirion like a young wild-ox."

144–145: Cf. Job 39:17; Jeremiah 51:3; Job 19:18.

150: Cf. 1 Kings 22:23: "The Lord hath put a lying spirit in the mouth of all these."

152: Cf. 2 Samuel 3:33: "Should Abner die as a churl dieth?"

154: Cf. Deuteronomy 28:7: "And shall flee before thee seven ways."

155: Cf. Psalms 109:20.

158: Cf. Numbers 19:15.

161: Cf. Isaiah 11:4: "And he shall smite the land with the rod of his mouth, and with the breath of his lips shall he slay the wicked"; Psalms 33:6: "By the word of the Lord were the heavens made, and all the hosts of them by the breath of His mouth."

162: Cf. Isaiah 38:12; Exodus 39:3.

165–166: Cf. 1 Samuel 2:6: "The Lord killeth and maketh alive; he bringeth down to the grave, and bringeth up"; Daniel 5:19: "Whom he [Nebuchadnezzar] would he slew, and whom he would he kept alive."

167–168: Cf. Isaiah 9:4; Deuteronomy 12:23.

169–170: Cf. Deuteronomy 28:56: "The tender and the delicate woman among you who would not adventure to set the sole of her foot on the ground for delicateness and tenderness"; and Isaiah 7:18–19: "And it shall come to pass in that day, that the Lord shall hiss for the fly that is in the uttermost part of the rivers of Egypt, And for the bee that is in the land of Assyria. And they shall come, and shall rest all of them in the rugged valleys, and in the holes of the rocks, and upon all thorns, and upon all brambles." Cf. *Gittin* 56a, for the story of Martha, the daughter of Boethius, who could not find flour during a time of famine in Jerusalem under the Romans. "When her servants failed to bring her even the crudest flour, she set out on her own. Some dung stuck to her feet and she died [from the shock]. Rabban Johanan b. Zakkai applied to her the verse [from Deuteronomy—above]."

171–172: Cf. Isaiah 53:5; Ezekiel 32:26; 1 Kings 13:24; Jeremiah 36:30.

173: Cf. 1 Samuel 26:20: "as when one doth hunt a partridge in the mountains"; Deuteronomy 1:44: "And chased you, as bees do."

177–178: Cf. Jeremiah 8:2: "And they shall be for dung upon the face of the earth"; Psalms 83:11; Zephaniah 1:17.

179–180: Cf. Ezekiel 40:16 and 29.

183–4: Cf. Isaiah 14:2; Jeremiah 30:16: "And all thine adversaries . . . shall go into captivity; And they that spoil thee shall be as spoil."

185–6: Cf. Psalms 44:6–7; 1 Samuel 17:45–47: "Then said David to the Philistine: 'Thou comest to me with the sword, and with the spear, and with the javelin; but I come to thee in the name of the Lord of hosts, the God of the armies of Israel, whom thou hast taunted.'"

190–1: Cf. Psalms 66:5, 28:4: "Give them according to their deeds, and according to the evil of their endeavors."

198: Cf. Isaiah 42:13.

200: Cf. Isaiah 16:11, 14:11.

202: Cf. Jeremiah 10:10.

205–6: Cf. Isaiah 41:2; Lamentations 3:16.

207–8: The second day of the week, when the battle began. In the year 1039, the second day of that week was Yom Kippur, and HaNagid's line ("the judgment was cast") refers to the liturgy for the Day of Atonement. The victory became apparent on the fifth.

210: Literally, "Arab and Philistine." Yarden notes that Philistine here refers to the Berbers. Cf. Ezekiel 25:16; Jeremiah 6:4.

212: The Hebrew involves a play on the word for "might" (*eitan*), the epithet for the autumn or late summer month of Tishrei (*ye'rach eitanim*—the moon of the mighty), and the biblical figure Eitan. HaNagid, like Eitan (Ethan), was a Levite. Eitan is identified in the Talmud with Abraham, the destroyer of idols; and the patriarchs Abraham, Isaac, and Jacob—the mighty men—were born in the month of Tishrei. Cf. 1 Kings 8:2; 1 Chronicles 6:27; *Baba Batra* 15a: "Ethan the Ezrahite is Abraham"; *Numbers Rabbah* 19:3: "Ethan is Abraham"; *Rosh Hashana* 11a: "R. Eliezer said: Whence do we know that the Patriarchs were born in Tishrei? Because it says, 'And all the men of Israel assembled themselves unto King Solomon, at the feast in the month of Eitanim, that is, the month in which the mighty ones [*eitanim*] of the world were born.'"

213: The Jewish year of 4799 came to a close at the end of Elul and the New Year began with the first of Tishrei.

215–16: Cf. Psalms 32:7: "Thou art my hiding-place; Thou wilt preserve me from the adversary. With songs of deliverance Thou wilt compass me about."

217: Cf. Exodus 15:12: "Thou stretchedst out Thy right hand—the earth swallowed them."

218: Cf. Isaiah 13:8.

219–222: Cf. Psalms 78:49; Psalms 29:8; Isaiah 13:5; Nahum 2:2; Job 38:28.

223–224: Cf. Psalms 116:13: "I will lift up the cup of salvation"; Isaiah 51:17; Zechariah 12:2.

225: Cf. Exodus 34:22.

227–228: Cf. Genesis 14:15; Exodus 11:4, 12:29, 12:22; and Joshua 10:13–14. Joshua made the sun and moon stand still until he had defeated the Amorites: "And there was no day like that before it or after it . . ." A phrase referring to "the night of the lifted burden" (Isaiah 10:27) or of the "redemption to come" (Fleischer) has been omitted from the English.

230–232: "Tent-dwellers" refers to Israel. Cf. Genesis 25:27: "Jacob was a quiet man, dwelling in tents. . . " The holidays mentioned are Rosh HaShana (the day of the shofar, or ram's horn), Yom Kippur (the Day of Atonement), and the pilgrimage festivals, which include Sukkot, or the Feast of Booths, Shavuot, or the Feast of Weeks, and Passover.

234: Cf. Jeremiah 20:9.

236: HaNagid did not want his men to fight on the Sabbath.

239–240: Cf. Proverbs 3:34: "If it concerneth the scorners, He scorneth them, but unto the humble He giveth grace." Jeremiah 3:15.

241–242: The people of Israel. Cf. Psalms 22:31–32, Psalms 102:19: "This shall be written for the generation to come; and a people which shall be created shall praise the Lord"; Isaiah 49:21.

246: Cf. Leviticus 23:40; Nehemiah 8:15: "And fetch . . . myrtle branches, and palm branches . . . to make booths."

247–248: Cf. Psalms 27:5: "For He concealeth me in the day of evil; He hideth me in the covert of His tent."

249–250: Cf. Isaiah 26:1: "We have a strong city; walls and bulwarks doth He appoint for salvation."

253–254: Cf. Nehemiah 8:15; Leviticus 1:3–4; Exodus 30:15.

255: Cf. Ezekiel 38:23.

256: Literally, "He became mighty over the water, in their involvement with the four that grow by the water." The "four species" traditionally associated with Sukkot are willow, palm, citron, and myrtle. Cf. Leviticus 23:40; Nehemiah 8:15; *Sukkah* 37a: "[For suppose] he could not find all the Four Species, he would be sitting and doing nothing while the Torah said, 'Ye shall dwell in booths for seven days,' implying a Sukkah of whatever material. And so with Ezra it says, 'Go forth unto the mount, and fetch olive branches, and branches of wild olive, and myrtle branches, and palm branches, and branches of thick trees to make Sukkoth. . .'"

257: Cf. Psalms 27:2: "When evil-doers came upon me to eat up my flesh . . . they stumbled and fell"; Psalms 20:9.

260–262: Cf. Genesis 28:12: "And behold a ladder . . . and behold the angels of God ascending and descending on it."

264: Cf. Job 21:17.

268: Cf. Joel 1:8.

269: Cf. Psalms 22:7: "But I am a worm, and no man; a reproach of men, and despised of the people."

271–272: Cf. 1 Samuel 18:18: "And David said unto Saul: 'Who am I, and what is my life?'"; 1 Samuel 25:3; Proverbs 20:11.

273–278: Cf. *Ta'anit* 20: "A man should never stand in a place of danger and declare, 'A miracle will befall me'; perhaps a miracle will not befall him. And if a miracle does befall him he suffers thereby a reduction from his merits. This can be inferred from the verse where it is written, 'I am not worthy of all the mercies, and of all the truth'" (Genesis 32:11). Cf. Psalms 18:21.

279–280: Cf. Psalms 24:8; Nahum 1:3: "The Lord is . . . great in power . . . the Lord, in the whirlwind and in the storm . . ."

281–282: Cf. Deuteronomy 32:17; Isaiah 42:8: "I am the Lord . . . and my glory will I not give to another, neither my praise to graven images."

283: Literally, "I've already set one *shira*" (poem or song—"The Battle at Al-fuente"—the second poem in his diwan, dated August 4, 1038).

284: Cf. Isaiah 13:10.

285–286: The Hebrew has 149 lines. According to an early Rabbinic account, the Book of Psalms once included 149 psalms. The standard masoretic text has 150.

286: Cf. The Arabic qasida on which HaNagid's verse was modeled consisted of independent monorhymed lines (called verses or stanzas in both Arabic and Hebrew) and the entire poem was compared to a necklace on which beads or pearls were strung.

Literally, "with the stones of song are measured." The lines refer to the quantitative meter of the poem.

293–294: Cf. Ezekiel 16:11–12: "I put bracelets upon thy hands . . . And I put a ring upon thy nose, and earrings in thine ears. . ."

296: Cf. Song of Songs 5:13: "His lips are as lilies, dropping with flowing myrrh"; Song of Songs 4:14; Proverbs 7:17.

301–302: Cf. Exodus 13:14: "And it shall be when thy son asketh thee in time to come, saying : 'What is this?'"

305: Cf. Job 28:27; Psalms 147:7.

THE DREAM (5)

The superscription and first line of the poem refer to the conspiracy by neighboring states against HaNagid, which is explained in the footnote to line 19 of "The

Victory Over Seville" (above). Ibn Abi Musa is another name for Ibn Bakanna, Malaga's military leader who is also referred to above (line 77, note). Although Ibn Abi Musa was Granada's ally against Seville, he resented HaNagid's position as a powerful Jew in a Moslem government and was anxious to see him removed. The grammar of the superscription is ambiguous in the original but seems to say that things went well for Ibn Abi Musa after Ben Abbas died, and that HaNagid had the dream in which he (HaNagid) read the poem. According to several accounts, Ibn Abi Musa died in battle shortly thereafter, an event HaNagid celebrated in poem #6 (not translated here).

The poem-composed-in-a-dream was a distinct category in medieval poetry, and Ibn Ezra devotes an entire chapter of his *Book of Remembrance and Discussion* to the convention: "Dreams which are seen with the dawn . . . are more true than most, announcing what will be before it occurs, on the condition that the man who sees that dream is truthful and gracious and restrained in his pursuit of carnal desire" (67a).

Line 4: Cf. Psalms 2:2: "The kings of the earth stand up, and the rulers take counsel together against the Lord, and against His anointed."
5: Cf. Isaiah 28:27: "But the black cumin is beaten out with a staff." Most references (*Berakhot* 40a among them) translate *ketzah* as "black cumin." One also finds "fennel" (the seed) or "love-in-a-mist."
7: Cf. Numbers 17:25.
8: Literally, "their evil and authority [or power]."

THE WAR WITH YADIR (7)

Yadir was a cousin of Granada's King Badis and aspired to his throne. The battle took place at Argona, which is east of Cordoba and north of Granada. Almuñekar, where Yadir was eventually imprisoned, is south of Granada, on the coast.

Line 1: Cf. Isaiah 22:4: "Therefore said I: 'Look away from me. . .'"
2: Cf. Proverbs 4:20, 2:2: "So that thou make thine ear attend unto wisdom and thine heart incline to discernment."
3–4: Cf. Psalms 27:1: "The Lord is my light and my salvation, whom shall I fear?"
7: Cf. Proverbs 5:9–10.
8–10: Cf. Jeremiah 33:9; Exodus 9:17: "As yet exaltest thou thyself against my people, that thou wilt not let them go?"
12: Cf. Ruth 1:18; Ezekiel 2:8: "Be not thou rebellious like that rebellious house"; 2 Chronicles 13:7.
16: Cf. Psalms 16:5: "O Lord, the portion of mine inheritance. . . . Thou maintainest my lot."

18: Cf. Psalms 62:8.

22: Cf. "A Day of Distress and Anguish," in which the archangels Gabriel and Micha'el appear to HaNagid. Also Exodus 18:4.

23: Cf. Leviticus 26:39.

24: Literally, "My fate is decreed from the heavens."

26: Literally, "there are people in life who never rule, like Tivni who died before his time, and Zimri." Cf. 1 Kings 16:10, 15–22.

28: Cf. Exodus 2:11.

29–30: Cf. Proverbs 13:23: "Much food is in the tillage of the poor: but there is that is swept away by want of righteousness."

32: Cf. Job 7:16: "Let me alone; for my days are vanity." Job 10:20, Job 21:13: "They spend their days in prosperity. . ."

33–35: Cf. Ezekiel 24:23; Proverbs 5:15: "Drink waters out of thine own cistern, and running waters out of thine own well"; Psalms 23:2: "He leadeth me beside the still waters"; Psalms 116:13.

36–37: Cf. Psalms 16:5 (as in line 16, above); Job 10:3.

38: Cf. Ezekiel 23:25.

40: Cf. Psalms 66:12: "We went through fire and through water. . ."

43–44: Cf. Psalms 17:11; Jeremiah 18:22: "They . . . have hidden snares for my feet." Psalms 9:16: "In the net which they hid is their own foot taken."

43–49: Cf. Isaiah 11:6. This stanza tries to mirror the complex weave of the Hebrew: *Ani evtach b'el hepil ashurai betoch pachim temanum leAshuri, b'yom ba tsar leIr meevtzar, vetavach betocho sar kemo egel v'cheemri. v'tsar zeh m'she'air malkhi—v'ra'at rechoki techsar mai'ra she'airi.*

50: Wasil and Muwafaq were the two princes.

51: Cf. Genesis 10:18 for the Zemarites, who were a Canaanite people. In this context, it refers to the Slavs. The city they siezed was Argona. According to Wasserstein, the Slavs were "people of largely Christian origin from non-Moslem ruled territories in Europe." The name derives from the Greek *sklavos*, for slave. Often mercenaries, they were a distinct population within the Andalusian mix and maintained their own communities.

52: The fortress (or forts) at Samantin, near the city of Jaen, 50 miles due north of Granada. Cf. Psalms 91:5–6: "Of the pestilence that walketh in darkness, . . . of the destruction that wasteth at noonday"; Deuteronomy 32:24.

57–61: Cf. Hosea 7:12; Isaiah 51:20; Job 39:18: "She raiseth her wings on high, and scorneth the horse and his rider." Isaiah 17:6: "Yet there shall be left therein gleanings, as at the beating of an olive-tree, two or three berries in the top of the uppermost bough, four or five in the branches of the fruitful tree, saith the Lord."

62: Cf. Isaiah 17:6. The long Hebrew vowel referred to here (*tseri*—pronounced "ai") has two dots side by side beneath a letter while the short one (*segol*—pronounced "eh") has three arranged in an inverted triangle beneath a letter.

65: Cf. Deuteronomy 1:4.

66: Cf. Leviticus 26:27.

69: Cf. Isaiah 18:7: "In that time shall a present be brought unto the Lord."

71: "My friend"—the same skeptical acquaintance to whom the opening of the poem is addressed.

82: Cf. 1 Samuel 12:11; Psalms 99:6; and *Rosh Hashana* 25b: "'Moses and Aaron among his priests and Samuel among them that call on his name.'. . . Jepthah in his generation [of his age] is like Samuel in his generation [of his age], to teach you that the most worthless, once he has been appointed a leader of the community, is to be accounted like the mightiest of the mighty."

83: Cf. 1 Samuel 10:11: "Is Saul also among the prophets?"

85–86: Cf. Exodus 6:16, 22–24. All of the people mentioned in these lines are descendants of Levi and therefore among the cult of the temple musicians. HaNagid reminds his listeners (as he does even more forcefully in the wine poem, "Have You Heard How I Helped the Wise?") that he too is a Levite.

89: Cf. Hosea 5:13: "He is not able to heal you, neither shall he cure you of your wound."

90: Cf. Psalms 39:1: "For Jeduthun. A psalm of David. . . ."

93–96: Cf. *Numbers Rabbah* 19: "'Then sang Israel'—Israel reasoned thus: It is Thy duty to perform miracles for us, and our duty to bless and praise Thy name." Also Psalms 55:15; Jeremiah 8:22.

97–98: Cf. Deuteronomy 24:14–15.

ON LIFTING THE SIEGE (II)

Lorca is some 120 miles northeast of Granada. It is located on the slopes of the Sierra del Cano and was one of the most famous fortresses in Andalusia. HaNagid's troops were sent to aid the city, which was under siege by Ibn Abi Ammar, the ruler of neighboring Almeria after the death of Zuhair.

Line 1: Schirmann notes that carrier pigeons had been used by the Greeks since the fifth century BCE, and references to them are common in medieval Spain. Habermann notes their appearance in Ibn Janakh (*Sepher HaRikmah* p. 316): "The dispatch of a bird with a message on the Sabbath is prohibited."

4: Cf. Song of Songs 3:6: "perfumed with myrrh and frankincense"; also Song of Songs 4:14.

10: Literally, "from the beam over the entrance." Cf. Proverbs 9:3.

12: Cf. Job 40:29: "Wilt thou play with him as with a bird?"

16–18: Cf. 1 Kings 22:17: "I saw all Israel scattered upon the mountains, as sheep that have no shepherd."

17: Cf. Hosea 13:3: "They shall be . . . as the chaff that is driven with the wind out of the threshing-floor."

19: Cf. Psalms 54:9, 58:11, 118:7.

20: Cf. Psalms 63:7, 90:4.

23–25: Cf. Psalms 69:7; Job 6:20: "They were ashamed because they had hoped; they came thither, and were confounded"; Jeremiah 2:26: "As the thief is ashamed when he is found . . "; Leviticus 25:29; Exodus 22:1.

26–28: Cf. Psalms 71:13, 109:29: "Mine adversaries shall be clothed with confusion, and shall put on their own shame as a robe"; Exodus 29:13.

29–30: Cf. Job 34:7; Ezekiel 23:33–34; Isaiah 51:17: "Thou hast drunken the beaker, even the cup of staggering, and drained it."

31–32: Cf. Jeremiah 4:31; Psalms 55:5; Jeremiah 6:24.

35: Cf. 1 Samuel 14:29.

36–37: Cf. Isaiah 65:14: "Behold, my servants shall sing for joy of heart, but ye shall cry for sorrow of heart and shall wail for vexation of spirit."

38–39: Cf. Isaiah 22:4.

40: Cf. 2 Samuel 22:2–3; Psalms 18:3: "The Lord is my rock . . . my high tower."

45–46: Cf. Deuteronomy 6:6–8: "And these words which I command thee this day, shall be upon thy heart; . . . thou shalt bind them for a sign upon thine hands [arms]"; Proverbs 3:3: "Write them upon the table of thy heart"; Job 19:24: "With an iron pen and lead they were graven in the rock forever."

YOUR MANUSCRIPT SHINES (8)

Sassoon's version of Yehosef's superscription reads: "And he commanded me, God honor him, to copy in my youth a certain book, and he promised to give me one *batil* (a coin) for each pamphlet that I completed, and he went off to one of the battles, and I sent him what I'd copied out for him. And he wrote me this:"

Line 2: Cf. Exodus 28:17; Ezekiel 28:13. The original is in dispute, Schirmann reading, literally, "like emerald arranged [in the High Priest's breastplate]" and Yarden reading "like emerald sapphired [or surrounded by sapphire]." The translation of the gem in question—*bareket*—is also uncertain (see "The Fawn"). I have worked for rhythmic and visual effect in my choices here.

3: Jonah 3:6.

7: Cf. Song of Songs 3:6: "perfumed with myrrh."

9–10: Cf. Exodus 25:21.

13: Cf. Job 19:24 (as above, "On Lifting the Siege," lines 45–46).

14–15: Cf. Exodus 29:13. Literally, "like a mark on my liver, not on its caul," i.e., a mark inside me, though not on the surface.

17–18: Cf. Jeremiah 4:19; Job 17:11.

19: Cf. Proverbs 27:5: "Better is open rebuke, than love that is hidden."

HaNagid speaks often of Yehosef in his poems, many of which were written while he was off on military business. Yehosef eventually joined his father for one campaign, when he was 9, but he grew homesick and soon was sent back to Granada. The event is recorded in Yehosef's only surviving poem, which Yehosef himself included in his copy of his father's diwan. Its superscription reads—"And I was taken with him when he went out on a mission to fight at a place nearby in the month of Nisan 1044 but my soul longed for my home and my loved ones and I wrote these four verses... and he helped me with them." Schirmann includes the poem in his anthology of *Hebrew Poems of Spain and Provence*, and notes that Yehosef, like his father, probably wrote poems about his battles and life at court, but these have been lost. Yehosef eventually inherited his father's position as Nagid and vizier. He was killed in a Granadan uprising in 1066 at the age of 31.

Line 1: Cf. Isaiah 5:28; Psalms 45:6 and 120:4; Isaiah 35:10.

3: Cf. Exodus 18:8; Numbers 20:14.

6: Cf. 2 Kings 8:29; Deuteronomy 28:59.

10–13: Cf. Isaiah 46:4; Job 6:12: "Is my strength the strength of stones? Or is my flesh of brass?"

16: Cf. Leviticus 13:20: "It is the plague of leprosy, it hath broken out in the boil"; Isaiah 1:14; Lamentations 1:13.

19: Cf. Job 33:19.

23: Cf. Jeremiah 8:23: "Oh that my head were waters, and mine eyes a fountain of tears, that I may weep day and night for the slain of the daughter of my people!"

26: Cf. Leviticus 13:20.

27–29: Cf. Ecclesiastes 12:3.

38–39: Cf. Exodus 28:36–38.

40: Cf. Psalms 126:3: "The Lord has done great things to us..."

41: Cf. Hosea 2:1.

44–45: Cf. Song of Songs 7:2; 2 Samuel 1:24.

49: Cf. Song of Songs 1:11: "We will make thee circlets of gold with studs of silver."

50: Cf. *Sotah* 9:14: "During the war against Vespasian they [the Rabbis] decreed against [the use of] crowns [or wreaths] worn by bridegrooms and against the use of the drum."

60: Literally, "read and write delightful writings." Cf. Isaiah 17:10.

61: Cf. Job 38:32.

64: Cf. Song of Songs 7:14.

65–66: Literally, "gloried among brothers." Cf. Genesis 49:26; Deuteronomy 33:16–17, 24.

The superscription refers to the journey described in poem 67, "On Fleeing His City." Osuna is a little more than 50 miles southwest of Cordoba, past the town of Ecija and across the River Genil. Marur, the Arabic name for the city of Morón, was further southeast. According to Ashtor, HaNagid here is speaking of an unusual winter campaign against Morón and Carmona, which had joined in an alliance against Granada. The Granadans were victorious, capturing cities and returning with spoils. A second round of fighting took place in the spring, with the Granadans again emerging victorious. These confrontations, instigated by the powerful king of Seville, Al-Mu'tadid, brought on a string of great victories and eventually led to a direct confrontation with Seville two years later. HaNagid, Badis, and the Granadan troops laid siege to the city but were unable to break through, and in time they retreated.

Line 1–4: "Pass" and "passed" are cognates in the Hebrew as well: *ma'avar* and *avri* (my passing). The Hebrew reads "fled with my walking stick," but the biblical inlay refers both to Genesis 32:10, where Jacob crossed the Jordan with his staff, and to the Aramaic Targum, which translates *"makli"* ("staff") as "alone." Onkelos, the second-century CE translator, understands the phrase to indicate "I did with nothing" or "I started from scratch." Rashi makes this clear in his comment to the passage: "I had with me neither silver nor gold nor cattle—only this staff of mine. The midrashic explanation is that he had placed his staff in the Jordan and the Jordan divided for him to pass over."

7–8: Cf. Job 29:23: "And they waited for me as for the rain"; Proverbs 7:24: "Attend to the words of my mouth."

9: Cf. Genesis 30:30: "And the Lord hath blessed thee withersoever I turned."

11: Cf. Hosea 11:4: "I drew them with cords of a man, with bands of love."

AMONG MY FRIENDS (36)

This battle poem also appears in the manuscript of *Ben Kohelet*. HaNagid was 61 when he wrote this and would live another two years.

Line 1–2: Cf. Proverbs 14:10: "The heart knoweth its own bitterness."

3–4: Cf. Exodus 3:22: "But every woman shall ask of her neighbor. . ."

6: Cf. Micah 1:8: "I will make a wailing like the jackals."

8–10: Cf. 2 Samuel 19:35; Ecclesiastes 2:8.

13: Literally, "Will time bring down and lay down the dew of youth on my herbs [or grasses]?" Cf. Job 37:11, 38:37; Isaiah 26:19; Exodus 16:14; 2 Kings 4:39.

14–16: Cf. Ecclesiastes 11:9.

19: Cf. Genesis 12:8.

23: Cf. Isaiah 10:16, 5:24.

24: Cf. Exodus 32:18; 2 Chronicles 21:15.

33: Cf. Exodus 27:3; Psalms 58:10.

36: Cf. Isaiah 10:32.

37–40: Cf. Proverbs 31:6; Isaiah 63:3.

43–45: Cf. Genesis 3:5: "Then your eyes shall be opened, and ye shall be as God"; Psalms 34:5; Isaiah 66:4. Literally, "the day of my fear," which is to say, "the day of death."

46–47: Cf. Genesis 2:7; Ezekiel 37:9.

49: Cf. Job 14:22: "But his flesh grieveth for him . . ."

50: Cf. Isaiah 1:6.

52: Cf. Psalms 103:5.

55–56: Cf. Psalms 73:28, 104:33: "I will sing unto the Lord as long as I live." Psalms 146:2, 5.

57: Cf. Job 3:12–17.

58: Literally, "And I worry lest I'll be confronted there by my rebelliousness [or sins]." Cf. Isaiah 59:13.

59: Cf. Genesis 15:15: "Thou shalt go to thy fathers in peace"; 1 Chronicles 17:11.

64: Cf. Genesis 19:8: "they are come under the shadow of my roof."

67–8: Cf. Joel 2:20.

71: Cf. *Avot* 4:22: "For not of thy will wast thou formed and not of thy will dost thou die, and not of thy will art thou to give just account and reckoning before the King of the kings of the kings, the Holy One, Blessed be He."

77–79: Cf. Psalms 33:6.

87: Cf. Job 30:23: "For I know that Thou wilt bring me to death, and to the house appointed for all living."

89: Cf. *Shabbat* 23:5: "And he who closes the eyes of a corpse at the moment the soul goes forth, lo, this one sheds blood"; Psalms 77:5.

92: Cf. Exodus 15:8: "The deeps were congealed in the heart of the sea." Exodus 15:16: "They are still as a stone."

93–95: Cf. Psalms 31:10: "Mine eye wasteth away with vexation, yea, my soul and my body"; Psalms 6:8; Zechariah 14:12: "and their eyes shall consume away in their sockets."

98: Cf. Proverbs 6:18.

99: Cf. Jeremiah 2:19.

102: Cf. Job 13:26.

103: Cf. Job 33:23–26: "If there be for him an angel, an intercessor . . . to vouch for man's uprightness."

109: Cf. Ecclesiastes 9:7: "For God hath already accepted thy works."

110: The manuscript here is hard to decipher. Schirmann reads, "And then you'll go down from my servants [prophets]," though this does not quite make sense. Yarden reads, "and thus my worthiness will go below my trans-

gressions [on the scales]." While there are problems with this as well, I have
followed Yarden.

112–113: Cf. Isaiah 58:8, 60:20, 5:30; and Psalms 136:7.

RISE EARLY (156)

In several respects one can say that medieval Hebrew secular poetry in Spain
begins with the wine poem, since the first well-known poem in the canon of the
new, Arabic-inspired quantitative verse is a wine poem by Dunash ben Labrat,
who had come to Spain from Abbasid Baghdad and introduced the Arabic poetic
practice to the Jewish literati in Andalusia. The Hebrew poets had ample opportunity to learn from models closer to home, as there were many important
Arabic poets in Andalusian Spain as well, but Dunash was clearly a driving force
in the translation of Arabic poetics into Hebrew. In his ground-breaking poem,
Dunash "invents" a courtier who begins by saying: "Don't sleep! Drink vintage
wine, bring henna and roses, and myrrh and aloes, in groves of pomegranates
and palms and grape vines. . . ." The description of the garden party continues
for some 15 lines and is then interrupted by the "I" of the poem, possibly Dunash—though the characterizations here, it would seem, are ambiguous by design. This person reproves the first speaker: "Silence! How could you talk of
these things while the house of holiness and the footstool of God are in the
hands of the gentiles. You have spoken foolishly and chosen sloth, you have
uttered nonsense . . . You have left behind reason and the Law of God Almighty.
How could you rejoice, while foxes run about in Zion?"

Although the poem expresses the ambivalent feelings that a poet like Dunash
may have had—and he was criticized for introducing various foreign elements
into Hebrew verse—the device of the interlocutor is also common in Arabic
poetry, so that in some respects even the "compunction" here is conventional.
At any rate, this is where it all begins, with Dunash's conflicted wine poem.

Generally speaking the conventions of the Arabic wine poem, as it came down
through sections of the classical ode and as it was developed in Abbasid verse by
poets such as Abu Nuwas, are taken over into Hebrew. As with the Hebrew love
poems based on Arabic models, the Hebrew wine poems are more temperate
than their Arabic precursors.

In the poem at hand, the image of gold and silver in the sky, and the black man
and white girl, are taken from Arabic poetry, though the Arab poets would often
specify the race or ethnic type they had in mind, e.g., Turks, Ethiopians, Copts,
Byzantines, Abyssinians, and so forth. The poet Ibn al-Mu'tazz (861–908) writes:
"Rise, while the night wrapped in its robe is like an Abyssinian fleeing its love."
Ali Ben Ali al-Hashim: "Look into the gloom of darkness, while the dawn comes
on, like a Byzantine army chasing the Abyssinians."

Lines 3–4: Alumunaftil, a Moslem contemporary of HaNagid, wrote: "Our night, when the morning comes after it, is like an Ethiopian chased by a Byzantine."

Line 4: Cf. Zechariah 6:3.

7–8: Abu Nuwas (c. 756–813, Basra, Baghdad), who is considered one of the great Arabic poets, was particularly renowned for his wine songs. They find numerous echoes in the poems of HaNagid: "As though [the wine] in his hand were the sun, and his hand the moon."

YOUR YEARS ARE SLEEP (130)

Line 1: Arabic literary tradition attributes a similar saying to the prophet Mohammed. Other versions of this idea appear in two Indian story collections, *The Prince and the Hermit*, in Ibn Hasdai's Hebrew translation—"As the wise man said: men while they live are asleep, and when they die, they wake"— and in *Kalila and Dimna* (see note to "Luxuries Ease," p. 216): "My soul, my soul, do not distance the morrow and rely on today, for your tomorrow is your awakening, and this day is your dream."

5: Cf. Psalms 68:36: "He giveth strength and power. . ."

6–8: Cf. *Haggigah* 13a: "And R. Aha b. Jacob said: There is still another Heaven above the heads of the living creatures, for it is written: 'And over the heads of the living creatures there was a likeness of a firmament, like the color of the terrible ice, stretched forth over their heads above' (Ezekiel 1:22). Thus far you have permission to speak, thenceforward you have not permission to speak, for so it is written in the Book of Ben Sira: 'Seek not things that are too hard for thee, and search not out things that are hidden from thee. The things that have been permitted thee, think thereupon; thou hast no business with the things that are secret.'"

11: Cf. 1 Samuel 16:17; Ezekiel 33:32; Psalms 46:1. The meaning of *alamoth* is uncertain. "Lute" is based on Yarden's reading: "an ancient musical instrument." It might also refer to one "who loves to sing [a certain kind of melody]."

12–13: Cf. Genesis 9:20–21: "And Noah, the husbandman, began and planted a vineyard." Abu Nuwas writes: "I asked the wine merchant: 'How long has it been since the presser pressed [them]?' He answered: 'This is beyond my powers of computation. They've told me that my grandfather's father chose it, from Adam's cellars, or Eve's.'" Another poem of his describes wine as follows: "This wine saw Noah, who was already old and gray, and it saw hundreds of years before Noah."

14: Cf. Job 28:18: "No mention shall be made of coral or of crystal; yea, the price of wisdom is above rubies."

20: Cf. 1 Chronicles 25:1–6. Jerimoth, the son of Heman.

24–26: Cf. Ecclesiastes 9:7. Koheleth is the preacher of Ecclesiastes and the Hebrew name for the book itself.

SAD FRIEND (157)

Line 1: Abu Nuwas: "I brought [the wine] water so that it will surrender to it. . ."

2–11: Abu Nuwas: "So that one will marry another / as the rain is husband to the vine." "They stood and mixed the wine with water / because the fruit of the two is joy."

HOW I HELPED THE WISE (131)

This poem departs from the conventions of a wine poem in many respects, and some scholars consider it a "boast" qasida, or poem of friendship. Again along lines of Arabic models, the wine here acts as a catalyst to the drinker's confidence and sets up the boast.

Lines 2–5: Abu Nuwas: "How pleasant is the party, which gathers nobles and high-born youths, generous, upright, and kind, their faces perfumed for their host, their voices pearls arranged in a row on his necklace." Or, "I chose men of truth, the choicest of men, the noble of nobles, patrons of patrons, and said: Enjoy! my heart and soul is yours to redeem, entertain yourselves all day long and all night until the crier calls."

7–9: Cf. Job 21:13, 36:11: "They shall spend their days in prosperity and their years in pleasure. . ."

8–9: Cf. Job 18:12: "Calamity shall be ready for his fall"; Jeremiah 20:10: "them that watch for my halting. . ."

10: Cf. *Ta'anit* 23a: "Raba said: Hence the saying, Either companionship or death."

14: Literally, "bowls full of precious things [or precious fruit]."

15: Literally, "in the hands of nobles clever [or wise] like us." Cf. Isaiah 32:5.

16: Cedars—Literally, "aloe-wood," though the precise meaning of the biblical term (*ahalim*) is uncertain. Scholars take it to mean the aloe tree, whose wood is used for incense and fumigation. The tree grows to 120 feet in height and 12 feet in girth. It is also possible that the term refers to a kind of cedar. In any event it is not the more familiar medicinal plant of the same name. Cf. Numbers 24:6; Psalms 45:9; Proverbs 7:17; Song of Songs 4:14.

18–19: *Eruvin* 65a: "R. Hiyya observed: He who retains a clear mind under the influence of wine possesses the characteristics of the seventy elders; for the numerical value of *yayin* (wine) is seventy and so is also the numerical [numerological] value of *sod* (counsel, or secret), so that when wine goes in, counsel departs." This phrase is sometimes interpreted in a more positive, mystical sense—"when wine goes in, secrets come out."

20–21: Literally, "And we sat in a goodly setting, and no one of heavy heart was there, and we did as we pleased." A common figure in Arabic poetry is the "heavy heart" or burdensome person, who is banished. Cf. Exodus 7:14.

22: Yuval (or Jubal) was "the ancestor of all who play the lyre and the pipe." Cf. Genesis 4:21: "And his brother's name was Jubal; he was the father of all such as handle the harp and pipe."

23: Cf. Psalms 150:4.

24: Cf. Exodus 25:33: "three cups made like almond blossoms. . ." Abu Nuwas writes: "And we passed the wine around in a cup with gold and precious gems."

25: Cf. Song of Songs 5:14: "His hands are as rods of gold set with beryl, his body is as polished ivory overlaid with sapphire"; Exodus 28:19.

28: Abu Nuwas: "Enclosed in a vessel, in the house of its sin, ninety years has been counted; it hasn't known the light of creation."

29–30: Cf. Genesis 38:6–9. When Tamar's husband, Er, died, the law required that his brother, Onan, take her as his wife. Onan, however, "spilled his seed" rather than impregnate his sister-in-law because the children would not have been his own. Tamar was wronged thereby.

31: The pitcher was like a woman with child. The wine was filtered and did not have any stems or seeds. Cf. Ecclesiastes 11:5: "how the bones do grow in the womb of her that is with child."

35: Cf. Job 33:21: "His flesh is consumed away. . ." Abu Nuwas: "Give me wine that was covered with a veil of age in the womb."

37–39: Cf. Song of Songs 3:6: "perfumed with myrrh and frankincense"; 2 Chronicles 16:14; Song of Songs 4:14; Ezekiel 1:27: "as the appearance of fire. . ." Abu Nuwas: "When the cup receives the wine, its scent seems seasoned, though you can't see the herbs." Abu Nuwas: "When we received the pure wine, it was like fire burning in the cup." Al-Mu'tazz: "When we mixed it, it was as though the water sent forth flame in the cup."

42: Tamim ben Ma'ad: "As though the beautiful clouds became for us cups, and as though the wine within them was lightning."

45: Abu Nuwas: "Ten years old, pure and refined, if it's poured on the night, the darkness disappears."

48: Abu Nuwas: "I strained my eyelids in fear of the view which was almost obliterated, because of [the sun's] light, when it rose."

49–51: Literally, "They held it—though it enticed them with the smoothness of its lips [or speech]." Cf. Proverbs 7:21.

53–54: Cf. Psalms 29:6: "He maketh them also to skip like a calf, Lebanon and Syrion like a young wild-ox."

55–56: Cf. Hosea 13:2; Jeremiah 13:19: "Judah is carried away captive, all of it, it is wholly carried away captive." Al-Mu'tazz: "I drink the wine and it drinks my knowledge." Abu Nuwas: "It flirts with men's minds before it smiles, but then it leads their wisdom astray."

57–61: Literally, "And they saw the poor man—and he ruled the adviser, and the fool; it had dominion over the wise, with its appearance, and good flavor, and fragrance." The English here takes a number of liberties. Cf. Job 29:8: "The young men saw me and hid themselves"; Psalms 119:6.

62: Cf. Lamentations 4:7: "They were more ruddy in body than rubies"; Leviticus 25:47.

66–67: An Arabic anecdote tells of a man who gave up wine, saying: "You send it to the stomach and it rises to the head."

70: Cf. Judges 4:21: "Then Jael, Heber's wife, took a tent pin and took a hammer in her hand, and went softly unto him [Sisera], and smote the pin into his temples"; Judges 5:26. Al'asha, a pre-Isalmic Arabic poet, describes the aftermath of a party as follows: "See the drunks scattered like nets spread for the monkeys." Isma'il ben Amar Alasdi (d. 774): "We set out toward the prayers slowly, without moving, as though our feet were being drawn out of clay."

74–75: Literally, "and they had in their necks no bones."

77: Cf. Zechariah 4:1: "And the angel that spoke with me returned, and waked me, as a man that is wakened out of his sleep."

83: Cf. Proverbs 9:3: "She calleth upon the highest places of the city. . ."

85–91: "The heir of Kehat": Kehat, one of the sons of Levi, i.e., I am a Levite (and therefore of distinguished lineage). Cf. Genesis 46:11, 6:4; 1 Samuel 1:1; Leviticus 18:6; Zephaniah 1:17.

86: Fleischer notes: "excellent taste" (for "craft").

92–95: Cf. Psalms 102:23: "When the peoples are gathered together. . ." Psalms 89:26–27: "He shall call unto Me, Thou art my Father. . ." Psalms 2:7: "The Lord said unto me: 'Thou art my son.'"

99: Cf. Psalms 68:36: "He giveth strength and power."

100–101: Literally, "[And I have] eloquence over the pleasing mouths [the temple singers], and stature well ahead of close-trimmed heads [the priests]." The translation here relies on Yarden's commentary.

102–103: Cf. Ezekiel 27:24: "chests of rich apparel."

104–105: Cf. Job 29:7–10: "The princes refrained talking, and laid their hands on their mouth. The voice of the nobles was hushed, and the tongue cleaved to the roof of their mouth."

109–110: Literally, "And even the wise and powerful who are very successful defer to me."

111: Cf. Proverbs 8:6: "I will speak excellent things. . . ." Literally, "And I reveal excellent things, and their matters were hidden [obscure or difficult]."

112: Literally "precious rhymes."

116: This line is in some dispute. Following Fleischer's note to poem 108 in the diwan, it would read, literally, "with all my ability none of my actions are angered." One might also read "bring about anger [in God]."

117–118: Literally, "And if I have sinned under compulsion or in secret, may God pardon [me] the compulsion and youthful exuberance [or the compelled and the hidden]." (See R. David Kimchi, *Sepher HaShorashim*, p. 267.)

ROUGE IN APPEARANCE (146)

Lines 2–3: Literally, "mixed in Espamya—and renowned [smelled] through India." Cf. Esther 1:1. "Espamya" is a rabbinic term for Spain, as opposed to the biblical "Sefarad." See *Nidah* 30b: "A person sleeping here [in Babylonia] might see a dream in Espamya."

5–6: Literally, "weak in its goblets [or vessel]." Cf. Song of Songs 7:3; Abu Nuwas: "Its power rises to heads and temples, as for its taste, it's like butter."

7–8: Cf. Deuteronomy 32:14; *Erubin* 65a: "R. Hanin observed: Wine was created for the sole purpose of comforting mourners and rewarding the wicked; for it is said, 'Give strong drink unto him that is ready to perish, and wine unto the bitter in soul. (Prov. 31:6–7)'". The tenth-century Damascene poet Abu Alfaraj Al-Wa'wa' writes: "Drink, by the flowers of the gardens, wine which banishes all worry with instant joy."

9–10: Cf. Joel 4:3; Obadiah 1:11; Nahum 3:10.

TAKE THE CRYSTAL (145)

Line 1: Cf. Deuteronomy 32:14: "Of the blood of the grape thou drankest foaming wine."

2–3: Abu Alfaraj Al-Wa'wa': "I chastised the wine in the mixing bowl / it smiled and hail appeared on the flame." Also in the 10th century, Al-Tanukhi writes: "The fawn carries water / in which flame flashes." Ibn Al-Mu'tazz (trans. Al-Udhari and Whightman): "You've seen a moonlit night silver the streets of a town; and wine pure as sunflecks, the glass turbanned with foam." *Midrash Rabbah* on Exodus comments on the biblical allusion (Exodus 9:24) "so there was hail, and fire flashing up amidst the hail: A miracle within a miracle. R. Yehuda and R. Nehemiah—one said—like the pomegranate seed, which can been seen within it. And the other said: Like an oil lamp, in which water and oil mix, while the light is lit from within them. What does this resemble? Two warriors who were fighting, and after a period the time came when the king called his soldiers to battle and made peace between them and sent them out together. So the fire and hail are hostile toward each other, but because the time had come to serve in battle for the king the Holy One Blessed Be He made peace between them and struck down the Egyptians."

4–5: Cf. Song of Songs 4:3: "Thy lips are like a thread of scarlet"; Song of Songs 7:10: "And the roof of thy mouth like the best wine. . ."

7: Cf. 2 Samuel 1:22: : "From the blood of the slain. . ."

8: A similar image is found in a poem by the 11th century poet Abu l-Hasan'Ali ibn Hisn: "Light passing through wine reflects the fingers of the cup bearer dyeing them red as juniper stains on the muzzle of the antelope" (trans. C. Franzen); Abu Nuwas: "Those of the stained fingertips were there . . ."; Ibn Al-Mu'tazz: "He gave me wine from the aged casks / the [boy] so handsome in his coquetry, whose fingertips were stained."

Ben Mishle

The 1197 Hebrew poems of *Ben Mishle* are arranged alphabetically, according to the first letter of each poem. Within this alphabetical order, the poems are then grouped by common meters. This is unusual in both Hebrew and Arabic verse from Spain, where the poems are normally arranged alphabetically according to the letter of their rhyme-scheme.

HaNagid does, however, employ a complicated variation of the latter principle (arrangement by rhyme-scheme): he introduces his book with a short poem, or motto, then arranges the penultimate consonant of the rhyme-syllables at the beginning of each of the twenty-two sections of the book (for the twenty-two letters of the Hebrew alphabet) so that they spell out the twenty-two words of the motto. For example, the first word of the motto is *Kechah* (take); the penultimate consonant in the rhyming syllable in the first poem of the first section (poems beginning with the letter *aleph*) is K: *rechoKim/shechaKim*. In the second *aleph* poem it is CH: *oo'voCHair/ le'aCHair*. In the third *aleph* poem the rhyme is on H: *gevoHim/haeloHim*. If you put the three penultimate consonants together the sounds spell out the word K-CH-AH: "Take," i.e., the first word of the motto. The same principle applies to the second word of the motto and the second section of the book (the poems beginning with the letter *bet*), and so on.

Ben Mishle was originally copied and arranged by HaNagid's youngest son, Eliassaf, who was born in 1049. In 1056, when Eliassaf was six and a half years old, HaNagid instructed him to begin work on the book. (According to Abramson, Eliassaf could read Torah by the age of three and a half.) It is not clear how long it took him to complete the task, though there is some indication that he may have finished before his father died (also in 1056).

As the preface indicates, many of the poems are taken from other languages and traditions. This was a common practice at the time and was not considered plagiarism, since the essence of the poem was in the poet's *treatment* of his conventional material. There was, however, engaged consideration of the problem of plagiarism in medieval Arabic and Hebrew literary criticism. While many parallels to Arabic proverbs are noted in some detail below, the reader might also be interested in the similarities between Ha-Nagid's work and that of the Greek poet Theognis (though Greek poetry was not part of the curriculum for Moslems and Jews at the time).

TRUTH IS HARD (1—in the Yarden edition)

Lines 1–4: Cf. Psalms 119:96: "I have seen an end to every purpose, but thy commandment is exceeding broad"; Job 11:5–9: "Sound wisdom is manifold! . . . Canst thou find out the deep things of God? Canst thou attain unto the purpose of the Almighty? It is high as heaven; what canst thou do? Deeper than the nether-world. . ."; *Avot* 2:15: "The day is short, the work formidable, the workers lazy, the wages high, the employer impatient"; Psalms 39:5; Esther 1:13; Ezekiel 12:27; Numbers 9:10; and Hippocrates: "Life is short / Art is long."

Lines 5–6: Cf. Exodus 32:34; Proverbs 12:2; Isaiah 33:5: "The Lord is exalted, for He dwelleth on high"; Deuteronomy 33:26: "Who rideth upon the heaven as thy help, and in His excellency on the skies."

Literally: "Lead your heart by them on the way that spreads the will of the dweller in the heavens."

WHEN THE LORD IS WITH YOU (5)

Line 1: Cf. Genesis 21:22: "The Lord is with thee in all that thou doest."

3: Cf. Deuteronomy 14:4–5.

4–6: From the Arabic epigram: "His teeth are set on edge / until he chokes on his spittle." The Hebrew also plays on the phrase *ya'ga la'reek* (to labor in vain), with *rok* (spittle) punning on *rek* (for nothing / in vain).

ONE WHO WORKS AND BUYS HIMSELF BOOKS (24)

Line 4: Literally, "empty and vain," or "empty and hollow." Cf. Ruth 1:21; Deuteronomy 15:13; Nehemiah 5:13; and *Pesachim* 5:6 (64a): "The Israelite killed [the lamb], and the priest caught [the blood]; he handed it to his colleague and his colleague [passed it on] to his colleague; and he received the full [basin] and gave back the empty one."

6: Cf. Ezekiel 23:14: "For she saw men portrayed upon the wall"; Ezekiel 8:10—Targum—"drawn."

8: Literally, "a hundred legs, then tries to get up, and can't." Cf. Ibn Khaldun's "introduction" to the study of history, *The Muqaddimah*, chapter 6, section 55: "A person who is ignorant of the composition of speech and its methods, as required by the (Arabic) linguistic habit, and who unsuccessfully attempts to express what he wants to express, is like an invalid who attempts to get up but cannot, because he lacks the power to do so."

HOW COULD YOU LOATHE (30)

Line 1–3: Cf. Psalms 90:8; Amos 6:8.
3–6: Cf. Jonah 1:12; 2 Samuel 13:4; Psalms 69:30: "I am afflicted and in pain."

FORGIVE THE MAN WHO SINNED AGAINST YOU (34)

Line 3–4: The last line plays on the words *psolet* (chaff or waste), and *solet* (fine flour). Cf. Genesis 41:3, 50:17, Amos 8:6; *Nedarim* 50b: "R. Gamada gave four *zuz* to sailors to bring him something. But as they could not obtain it, they brought him a monkey for it. The monkey escaped, and made his way into a hole. In searching for it, they found it lying on precious stones, and brought them all to him. The Emperor's daughter said to R. Joshua b. Hananiah: 'Such comely wisdom [instruction] in an ugly vessel!' He replied, 'Learn from thy father's palace. In what is the wine stored?' 'In earthen jars,' she answered. 'But all [common] people store wine in earthen vessels, and thou too likewise! Thou shouldest keep it in jars of gold and silver!' So she went and had the wine replaced in vessels of gold and silver, and it turned sour. 'Thus,' said he to her, 'The Torah is likewise!' 'But are there not handsome people who are learned too?' 'Were they ugly they would be even more learned,' he retorted."

IF YOU'RE FINDING THE GOOD AT FAULT (51)

Lines 1–2: Literally, "If you're finding the good are harmful," i.e., "if you think the good are against you." Cf. Isaiah 9:1: "The people that walked in darkness have seen a great light"; Ecclesiastes 2:14: "the fool walketh in darkness"; Isaiah 29:15.
3: Literally, "If you can't acknowledge. . ." Cf. Jeremiah 24:5.

DELAY YOUR SPEECH (54)

Line 1: Cf. Genesis 24:56: "He said unto them: 'Delay me not.'"
3: Cf. Proverbs 4:25; Job 5:24; literally, "and not sin."
4: Job 41:20; 1 Samuel 31:3; 1 Chronicles 10:3.
6: Cf. Judges 20:16; Deuteronomy 8:8. The poem plays on the similarity between *yehtai* (to sin) and *hitta* (wheat). Cf. *Berakhot* 61a: "Samuel said: [The evil incli-

nation] is like a kind of wheat [*hitta*], as it says, sin [or deceit—*hattat*] circleth at the door" (Genesis 4:7). This is probably in connection with the notion that the forbidden food of which Adam ate was wheat. See *Berakhot* 40a.

I'D SUCK BITTER POISON FROM THE VIPER'S MOUTH (58)

Lines 1–2: Cf. Job 20:14–15: "The food in his bowels is turned; it is the gall of asps within him"; Isaiah 11:8: "And the sucking child shall play on the hole of the asp, and the weaned child shall put his hand on the basilik's den." The second line in the original reads, "And to the hole of the children of vipers I'd be led to dwell."

3–4: Cf. Proverbs 23:6; Deuteronomy 2:28; Numbers 20:19; Proverbs 17:1; 2 Samuel 12:3.

The third line in the original reads, "And not pass through on my feet near churls." The last line reads, "And not eat a morsel of bread of the vile." The verb for "eat" puns on the verb for "fight" and "bread" in the Hebrew (l-ch-m).

IF YOU DON'T HAVE THE POWER TO PAY (75)

Cf. The Arabic epigram from the *Alikkad Alfarid*, an encyclopedia of Arabic poetry and prose, edited by Ibn Abbad Rabbah of Cordoba (c. 940): "It is better for man to pardon one with his power than it is to punish all."

Line 1: Cf. Psalms 94:2: "Render to the proud their recompense."

2: Cf. Genesis 50:17: "So shall ye say unto Joseph: 'Forgive . . . the transgression of thy brethren, and their sin, for that they did unto thee evil.'" Psalms 132:1. Literally: "Forgive what they did to your soul in your affliction."

3: Literally, "you're a man of strength." Cf. Judges 8:21.

4: Cf. Psalms 79:9, 78:38; Leviticus 5:13.

HE WHO LINGERS AT THE COURT OF THE KING (84)

Line 2: Cf. Isaiah 9:4; Psalms 64:3; Jeremiah 11:16: "with the noise of a great tumult."

3: Literally, "And isn't vexed by the provocation he sees." Cf. 2 Kings 23:26: "Wherewith His anger was kindled against Judah, because of all the provocations wherewith Manasseh had provoked him. . . ."

4: Cf. Proverbs 2:16: "the alien woman that maketh smooth her words"; Genesis 4:23.

5: Literally, "his wishes will be fulfilled." Cf. Psalms 20:6. Cf. *Kalila and Dimna*

95 (see note to "Luxuries Ease," p. 216.): "No one can persevere at the king's gate unless he has put anger behind him and bears (with patience) insult, and conquers his anger, and learns to befriend people and keep a secret; if he can do this, he has already gained what he seeks." Ibn Qutaiba: "And I read in it [the book of the Indians]: Who clings to the king's gate with refined patience and refrains from anger . . . will get what he desires." There is also a Talmudic play on the word *sa'on* (noise or stomping) and *se'ah* (measure): Cf. Sotah 8:b.

IN BUSINESS DON'T GET INVOLVED (92)

Line 1: Cf. Nehemiah 10:32.
2: Cf. Proverbs 20:19: "Meddle not with him that openeth wide his lips."
3: Cf. Isaiah 57:19.

IF YOU SHAME A MAN (98)

Line 1: Cf. Hosea 2:7: "She that conceived them hath done shamefully."
3–4: Literally, "for the hidden flaws your heart knows of." Cf. *Kiddushin* 11a: "bodily defects [or flaws] that are apparent . . . bodily defects [or flaws] that are hidden."

PEOPLE WELCOME THE RICH (118)

Line 1–4: Cf. Proverbs 14:20: "The poor is hated even of his own neighbor; but the rich hath many friends." Ben Sira 13:21–23 (New Oxford Annotated Bible): "When a rich man slips, his helpers are many; he speaks unseemly words, and they justify him. If a humble man slips, they even reproach him; he speaks sensibly, and receives no attention. When the rich man speaks all are silent, and they extol to the clouds what he says. When the poor man speaks they say, 'Who is this fellow?' And should he stumble, they even push him down."
3–4: Job 34:6: "My wound is uncurable, though I am without transgression."

HE WHOSE HEART IN HIS HEART (123)

Line 1–2: Cf. 2 Chronicles 17:6: "And his heart was lifted up in the ways of the Lord. . ."; Leviticus 4:10; Exodus 29:27.
3: Cf. Psalms 68:27. Literally, "and isn't lifted up in the assemblies."
5–6: Cf. Psalms 99:5; Jeremiah 13:17; Ezekiel 21:29: "Because ye have made your iniquity to be remembered, and that your transgressions are uncovered, so that your sins do appear. . ."

IF YOU LEAVE A LONG-LOVED FRIEND (126)

RESPECT AND DISCRETION (141)

Line 1–4: Proverbs 12:9; 2 Samuel 6:22; Judges 11:9; Jeremiah 51:27; *Sanhedrin* 7a: "There was a man who used to say: Happy is he who hears abuse of himself and ignores it; for a hundred evils pass him by." Also, *Shabbat* 88b: "Our rabbis taught: Those who are insulted but do not insult, hear themselves reviled without answering, act through love and rejoice in suffering, of them the Writ saith, 'But they who love Him are as the sun when he goeth forth in his might (Judges 5:31).'"

5–8: Cf. Proverbs 18:2: "The fool does not desire understanding, but only to air his thoughts" (NJPS); Job 22:9; Ecclesiastes 4:8.

THE RICH ARE SMALL (173)

YOU WHO'D BE WISE (195)

Lines 1–2: Cf. *Avot* 4:1: "Who is wise? He who learns from every man"; Ecclesiastes 7:16; *Berakhot* 63b: "R. Ishmael says, One who desires to be wise should occupy himself with money judgments, since no branch of Torah surpasses them, for they are like a perpetual fountain [of instruction]."

3–4: Literally, "righteousness and wickedness." Cf. Proverbs 10:8–9, 11:5.

WHEN YOU'RE DESPERATE (198)

Line 1: Cf. Judges 6:6: "And Israel was brought very low."

6: Cf. Psalms 78:40. Yarden notes a parallel text from Arabic (*Alrisala Alqasira*): "Traces of envy will show up in you before they show up in those who hate you."

IT'S HEART THAT DISCERNS (231)

Line 1: Cf. 1 Kings 3:9: "Give Thy servant therefore an understanding heart to judge . . . that I may discern between good and evil."

3: Cf. Proverbs 15:32, 19:8.

5–6: Cf. Jeremiah 1:10: "See, I have this day set thee over the nations . . . to root out and to pull down, and to destroy and to overthrow, to build, and to plant"; *Megillah* 31:b: "R. Simeon b. Eleazar says: If old men say to you, 'throw down,' and young men say to you, 'build up,' throw down and do not build up, because destruction by old men is construction, and construction by boys is destruction; and the example is Rehoboam son of Solomon [who destroyed his power by following the advice of the young men which was intended to strengthen it—1 Kings 12]." Literally, "and think their destruction a building."

STAB YOUR HEART (290)

Line 1: Cf. *Gittin* 56b: "Vespasian sent Titus who said, 'Where is their God, the Rock in whom they trusted?' This was the wicked Titus who blasphemed and insulted Heaven. What did he do? He took a harlot by the hand and entered the Holy of Holies and spread out a scroll of the Law and committed a sin on it. He then took a sword and slashed the curtain. Miraculously blood spurted out, and he thought that he had slain himself. . ."; Psalms 95:4.

3: Cf. Proverbs 26:3: "A whip for the horse, a bridle for the ass, and a rod for the back of fools."

4: Cf. Proverbs 14:4; Judges 3:31: "And after him was Shamgar . . . who smote of the Philistines six hundred men with an ox goad."

IS THERE ANY FRUSTRATION (375)

Cf. The Arabic anthology *Alikkad Alfarid:* "And it was said to the Arab: Who in creation deserves mercy? And he said: The generous man (or patron) who is ruled by a cruel (or vile) man and the kind man who is ruled over by a fool."

Line 2: Cf. Job 9:4.

3: Cf. Isaiah 44:12: "Yea, he is hungry, and his strength faileth." Numbers 30:6, 32:7; Lamentations 4:17.

4: Cf. Isaiah 32:5.

DID YOUR FATHER LEAVE YOU GLORY (377)

Line 2: The beginning of this line can be translated also as "repair." Cf. Nehemiah 4:1; 2 Chronicles 24:13: "So the workmen wrought, and the work was perfected by them."

4: Literally, "And you'll be a father for those who come after you."

COULD KINGS RIGHT A PEOPLE GONE BAD (382)

Line 1: Cf. Proverbs 4:25; Habakkuk 1:4: "Therefore the law is slack, and right doth never go forth; for the wicked doth beset the righteous; therefore right goeth forth perverted. . . "

2: Cf. Deuteronomy 32:5: "a generation crooked and perverse"; 2 Samuel 23:20.

3: Cf. Numbers 23:27; Ecclesiastes 1:15: "That which is crooked cannot be made straight. . ."

4: Cf. Lamentations 3:9: "He hath enclosed my way with hewn stone, he hath made my paths crooked."

THE KING (413)

Yarden quotes the Arabic proverb attributed to Sahl ibn Harun: "The ruler has the qualities of the drunk, among them to be pleased with one who deserves his anger and to be angry at one with whom he should be pleased."

HE'LL BRING YOU TROUBLE (632)

Line 1: Cf. 2 Kings 9:11.

2: Cf. Psalms 137:3: "For there they that led us captive asked of us words of song, and our tormentors asked of us mirth: 'Sing us one of the songs of Zion'"; Judges 5:12: "Awake, awake, Deborah . . . utter a song."

3: Literally, "My son, not every dream is realized [or comes true]." Cf. Zechariah 10:2; Ecclesiastes 5:6: "Through the multitudes of dreams and vanities there are also many words. . ."

4: Literally, "Not everything is true that the poet says." Cf. Aristotle (*Metaphysics* 982b and *Poetics* 24:9), to whom Ibn Ezra refers in *The Book of Remembrance and Discussion* when he says, "all images [metaphors] lie." The version here plays on the three-word Arabic proverb, "The-best of-a-poem is-its-falseness," which was central to the poetics of the Spanish-Hebrew writers of the period as well. Note also Ibn Ezra (*The Book of Remembrance and Discussion* 64a): "The poet is he who most skillfully draws a form that will astonish the eye and yet not have substance."

Also, Al-Buhtri (d. 897): "You have imposed the rules of your logic upon us; lying in poetry supersedes truthfulness."

THE WISE UNDERSTAND (799)

Line 1: Cf. Ezekiel 21:5: "Is he not a maker of parables?"; Job 9:4.

3–4: Cf. Ecclesiastes 10:14. Literally, "And the fool can't understand parables, even if they're slight, until you've used a lot of words."

ASSISTANTS COME TO JUDGMENT IN GROUPS (892)

Line 1: Cf. Ezra 9:2; Psalms 122:5.

2: Cf. Genesis 19:1; *Sanhedrin* 8a: "R. Johanan said: Moses said to Joshua: Thou shalt be like the elders of the generation that are among them. But the Holy One, Blessed be He, said to Joshua: Take a stick and strike them upon their head; there is only one leader to a generation, not two. . . "

3: Cf. Psalms 127:4–5.

4: Cf. Ezekiel 21:10: "And all flesh shall know that I the Lord have drawn forth My sword out of its sheath."

THE GOOD STUDENTS TEND (894)

Line 1–3: Cf. *Avot* 1:16: "Get yourself a master and remove yourself from what is doubtful and do not tithe by conjecture"; Deuteronomy 29:28: "The secret things belong unto the Lord our God, but the things that are revealed belong unto us"; Esther 3:14.

3–6: Cf. Isaiah 3:3: "the cunning charmer and the skilful enchanter"; Proverbs 20:5: "Counsel in the heart of man is like deep water, but a man of understanding will draw it out."

WHAT'S FAMILIAR IS SOMETIMES DISTANCED (962)

Line 1: Literally, "Sometimes things are distanced from you that had been brought close, and [things are] brought close [that were] far."

2: Cf. Ben Sirach 13:10: "Do not push forward lest you be repulsed, and do not remain at a distance lest you be forgotten."

3: Cf. Proverbs 13:13; Leviticus 11:4; Ezekiel 32:13.

4: Literally, "will fall into deep water." Cf. Proverbs 20:5.

THE HEART HOLDS HIDDEN KNOWLEDGE (970)

Line 1: Cf. Psalms 139:6: "Such knowledge is too wonderful for me; too high, I cannot attain unto it."

FIRST WAR (1034)

The poem is based on the Arabic attributed to Imru al-Qais (500–542): "War [at first] is a beautiful girl urging young men to sign away their lives. As the fire breaks into flames she becomes a headless hag who offers a broken promise and an [unkissable] stinking corpse." Al-Ma'ari (973–1057) has an interesting twist on this: "If the intellect is unstable / it is overwhelmed by the world, / a weak man embraced by a whore. / If the mind becomes disciplined, / the world is a distinguished woman / who rejects her lover's advances." (Both translations A. al-Udhari.)

SOAR, DON'T SETTLE (1097)

Line 1: Literally, "Don't stand between earth and sky." Cf. Psalms 57:12: "Be thou exalted, O God, above the heavens"; 2 Samuel 18:9: "And he [Absolom] was taken up between the heaven and earth; and the mule that was underneath"; Jeremiah 51:9.

2: Literally, "soar to the Bear" (the constellation).

3: Cf. Deuteronomy 31:7: "Be strong and of good courage. . ."; 1 Kings 18:5.

4: Cf. Isaiah 53:4; Job 4:11.

COMMERCE HAS MARKETS (1118)

Line 1–7: Cf. *Tanhuma b'Hukotai, Eshkol*, 634–35: "Asked Rabbi Shmuel Bar Nahmani of Rabbi Yonatan Bar Elazar who was standing in the market, he said to him: Teach me a chapter. He said to him: Go to the house of study and I'll teach you there. . . Where are pearls and precious stones sold?. . . Where the markets are. . . . So it is with the Torah." See also *Baba Metzia* 24b: "Raba once followed R. Nahman into a street [market] of skinners—some say a street [market] of scholars."

1: Cf. Song of Songs 3:2; Leviticus 25:14; Ezekiel 38:12.

2: Cf. Psalms 107:32: "Let them exalt Him . . . in the assembly of the people and praise Him in the seat of the elders."

7: Cf. Ezekiel 28:13.

THREE THINGS (1127)

Line 1–6: Cf. The Arabic of Ibn Hamdun (quoted in Yarden): "There are three things a man cannot achieve without the help of superior ambition and great risk: the service of kings, maritime trade, and war with the enemy."

1: Literally, "Each who'd risk his life. . ." Cf. *Berakhot* 11a: "I was on my way . . . and I endangered [risked] myself before the robber."

2: Literally, "All who'd raise their hearts." Cf. 2 Chronicles 17:6.

4: Cf. Isaiah 45:14.

THE FOOLISH ENEMY'S FACE TELLS ALL (1145)

Line 1–4: Cf. Isaiah 3:9; *Ketubot* 111b: "He who shows the whiteness of his teeth to his friend is better than he who gives him milk to drink, as it is said: His teeth are whiter than milk (Genesis 49:12)."

2: Literally, "plays (or acts) with you." Cf. Psalms 104:26; Job 40:29.

Line 3: Cf. Esther 5:2–3: "And it was so, when the king saw Esther the queen standing in the court, that she obtained favor in his sight; and the king held out to Esther the golden sceptre that was in his hand. So Esther drew near, and touched the top of the sceptre. Then said the king unto her: 'What wilt thou, Queen Esther? for whatever thy request . . . it shall be given thee.'"

Ben Kohelet

As in *Ben Mishle*, the 411 poems in the Hebrew manuscript of *Ben Kohelet* are arranged alphabetically by the first letter of each poem. Within that arrangement the poems are further organized by their meters, and once again Ha-Nagid weaves the consonants of his motto through the rhymes of the twenty-two sections of the book (except for the letters *aleph* and *chet*, where poems may be missing).

The poems are presented without preface, and their editor is unknown. In his introduction to the Oxford edition, Sassoon suggests that HaNagid himself arranged the poems. Habermann suggests it was HaNagid's older son, Yehosef. Abramson says that we do not know enough to suggest an editor, that perhaps the copyist simply omitted the preface at some point. He leans, however, toward HaNagid as the most likely candidate.

Several poems appear in both *Ben Kohelet* and *Ben Tehillim* or *Ben Mishle*, or as parts of poems in those books. Generally, I have tried to group the poems by tone and subject, and where poems overlap, for the most part I have placed what seem to be the later poems in *Ben Kohelet*. It should be pointed out, however, that the date of the book's completion is not known. Whereas the superscriptions to *Ben Tehillim* often include the date of a given poem, there are neither superscriptions nor dates in the extant manuscripts of *Ben Kohelet*.

The first mention of this book in later literature is by Moshe Ibn Ezra in *The Book of Remembrance and Discussion*: "And it [*Ben Kohelet*] is the most sublime and admirable of HaNagid's compositions, and it is more beautiful and more profound than *Ben Tehillim* and *Ben Mishle*, because it was written after its author reached middle age."

GAZING THROUGH THE NIGHT (22—in the Abramson edition)

This poem appears in both *Ben Kohelet* and *Ben Tehillim*. In the latter it is incorporated into a poem of friendship, beginning: "It's upon you, sons and supporters of the Law, it's upon you to reveal its secrets, because humankind upon earth is in darkness, and you are its sun."

Lines 1–5: Cf. Psalms 8:4: "When I behold Thy heavens, the work of thy fingers, the moon and the stars. . ."; Psalms 104:24; *Berakhot* 10a: "He came out into the open air [of the world] and looked upon the stars and constellations and broke into song."

3–4: Literally, "the earth and its creeping things." Cf. Genesis 1:25–6: "every thing that creepeth upon the ground." Rashi's annotation to Genesis 1:25 reads: "It [*remes*] means creeping swarms that creep low upon the ground; they appear as though they are dragged along, for how they move is not discernible." Genesis 6:7: "Man and beast and creeping things, and fowl of the air." Also, Ha-Nagid's contemporary Ibn Hazm (994–1064): "If I should come to possess [love], then all the earth will [seem like] a senile camel and mankind motes of dust, while the land's inhabitants will [seem like] insects" (trans. J. Monroe).

8: Cf. Isaiah 40:22: "It is He . . . that stretcheth out the heavens as a curtain, and spreadeth them out as a tent to dwell in." *Baraita de Shmuel HaKatan* 1: "The heavens are made like a tent."

9: Cf. Exodus 26:4ff., which describes the sanctuary in the desert: "And thou shalt make loops of blue upon the edge of the one curtain. . ."; *Shabbat* 99a: "the clasps in the loops looked like stars set in the sky." The Arabic poet Ibn Tabataba wrote: "As though the sky wore the night like a studded dress sewn to measure, and inlaid with gems on every side, fastened in the air with buttons."

10: Cf. Psalms 8:4, as above, lines 1–5.

11–13: Cf. Ibn Gabirol, "KeShoresh Etz" (Brody-Schirmann, poem 203), "And he sent his stars about like a shepherd sending forth his flock into the fields." This is also a common image in Arabic poetry.

14–15: Cf. Jeremiah 10:13; Proverbs 25:14. Schirmann reads "clouds;" Yarden, "clouds carried by wind." The biblical reference alludes to "vapours." Ibn al-Mu'tazz compares the moon to a ship of silver loaded with amber incense; other poets use the image of a ship as well.

19–21: Cf. Isaiah 18:4: "a cloud of dew." "Shaking water"—the Hebrew plays on the root n-a-r: *na'arah tena'air*, (a girl—*na'arah*—will shake out—*tena'air*) then alludes to Song of Songs 5:2: "For my head is filled with dew, My locks with the drops of the night." I have taken several liberties here to establish a similar weave in the English

22: Some versions of the text have two extra lines here. See Yarden, *Ben Tehillim* (poem 41). Cf. Isaiah 18:3: "All ye inhabitants of the world, and ye dwellers on the earth. . ."

24: The Hebrew (*hayyah*) is in dispute, and Abramson discusses the matter in his notes to *Ben Kohelet*. Both he and Yarden read "troops," alluding to 2 Samuel 23:13: "the troops of the Philistines." The word might also mean "beast." Schirmann does not comment here. A literal version of the entire passage would read: "And dwellers on earth are like beasts falling off to sleep [or troops pitching camp for a night], our yards/courts their stalls."

25: Literally, "as all will flee from the fear of death, like a dove which a hawk pursues."

27: Cf. *Mekhilta BeShallach* III: 86: "To what were the Israelites at that moment like? To a dove fleeing from a hawk."

28–29: Cf. Isaiah 30:14: "And He shall break it as a potter's vessel is broken, breaking it in pieces without sparing; so that there shall not be found among the pieces thereof a sherd;" 2 Kings 21:13: "And I will wipe Jerusalem, as a man wipeth a dish"; *Baba Batra* 16a: "Raba said: Job sought to turn the dish upside down [to declare all God's works worthless]"; *Pesachim* 50a: "Rabbi Joseph the son of R. Joshua b. Levi became ill and fell into a trance. When he recovered, his father asked him, 'What did you see?' 'I saw a topsy-turvy world, the upper [class] was underneath and the lower on top.' 'My son,' he observed, 'you saw a clear world.'" The image of the broken plate is common in Arabic poetry, e.g.: "Death will smash us into pieces as though we were glass." (Abu Al-Ala Al-Samari).

LOVERS OF LIFE (14)

Line 1: Literally, "Did you know your lives are pointless?" Abramson suggests the alternate reading of *ohavei hayyim* (lovers of life) for *ohavei yamim* (lovers of days). Cf. Psalms 34:13: "Who is the man that desireth life, and loveth days, that he may see the good therein?"

THE MULTIPLE TROUBLES OF MAN (24)

Line 1–2: Cf. Exodus 18:8; Psalms 71:20: "Thou, who hast made me to see many and sore troubles. . . ." Also *Hagigah* 5b. The Hebrew has *betsarot* ("in trouble" or "in pain"); Abramson suggests *ketsarot* ("like troubles" or "like pain"), which I have followed.

3: Cf. Genesis 43:33.

BE GLAD, SHE SAID (35)

Lines 8–9: Cf. Ibn Hazm: "Having seen the hoariness on my temples and sideburns, someone asked me how old I was. I answered him: I consider all my life to have been but a short moment and nothing else. . ." (trans. J. Monroe).

EARTH TO MAN (38)

Line 2: Jeremiah 37:4, 52:31.
Cf. Al-Ma'ari: "We're surrounded by a place from which escape is impossible, and time is running out on its souls [residents]."

YOUR LOVED ONES DEPRESS YOU (65)

Line 3: Cf. Leviticus 19:17.
7–10: Literally, "For your loss (death) is in your sin, and your life in goodness."
9–10: Literally, "Fight in your soul. . ." Cf. *Berakhot* 5:a: "R. Levi b. Hama says in the name of R. Simeon b. Lakish: A man should always incite the good impulse [in his soul] to fight against the evil impulse. For it is written: 'Tremble and sin not' (Psalms 4:5)"; Deuteronomy 30:15.
11: Cf. Deuteronomy 13:7: ". . . or thy friend, that is as thine own soul, entice thee secretly. . ."
13: Literally, "the Lord is in the midst of thee." Cf. Zephaniah 3:17.

SOUL OPENS INSIDE YOU (66)

Line 3: Literally, "and it hides its flaws." Joshua 6:17.
4: Cf. Genesis 3:22; Deuteronomy 32:40.
5–6: Cf. Psalms 102:21.

THE CHILD AT ONE OR TWO (79)

A classic "stages of life" text. Cf. *Avot* 5:21: "He would say: At five to [the study of] Scripture, ten years to Mishnah, thirteen to the commandments, fifteen to Talmud, eighteen to the [wedding] canopy, twenty to pursuit [of a livelihood], thirty to [fullness of] strength, forty to understanding, fifty to counsel, sixty to old age [maturity], seventy to grey hair, eighty to 'extended strength,' ninety to [a] bending [figure], at one hundred he is as though he were dead, and had passed away and faded from the world." Cf., also, *As You Like It*, Act II, Scene 7: "All the world's a stage. . ." and the seven ages of man.

2: Cf. Jeremiah 8:17: "I will send serpents and basilisks among you. . ." The 1917 JPS translation has "serpents, basilisks" for *tsiphoneh nachashim*; the RSV has "serpents, adders." Also Isaiah 11:8: "And the sucking child shall play on the hole of the asp, And the weaned child shall put his hand on the basilisk's [viper's] den." *Ecclesiastes Rabbah* 1:4—"R. Samuel b. R. Isaac taught in the name of R. Samuel b. Eleazar: The seven *'vanities'* mentioned by Koheleth correspond to the seven worlds a man beholds. At one year old he is like a king seated in a canopied litter, fondled and kissed by all. At two and three he is like a pig, sticking his hand in the gutters. At ten he skips like a kid. At twenty he is like a neighing horse, adorning his person and longing for a wife. Having married, he is like an ass. When he has begotten children, he grows brazen like a dog to supply their food and wants. When he has become old, he is [bent] like an ape."

3–4: Cf. Song of Songs 2:8: "Hark! My beloved! Behold, he cometh, leaping upon the mountains, skipping upon the hills."

7: Cf. Ecclesiastes 11:10.

9: Literally, "he becomes righteous (blameless) and joins his friends the elders." The implication is that he matures and comes to completion of character. Cf. Psalms 18:26.

12: Literally, "the whitening of his head and beard."

13–14: Cf. Job 24:17: "For they know the terrors of the shadow of death."

15–16: Cf. Genesis 48:10. Abramson notes that the manuscript here is hard to decipher and he reads *nireh* (seems/appears) rather than *nikheh* (is broken).

17–18: Cf. Job 18:10; Hosea 9:8: "As for the prophet, a fowler's snare is in all his ways." Also Psalms 91:3, 124:7.

20: Literally, "He won't know the harvest [season] from the ploughing [season]." Cf. Genesis 45:6.

22: Cf. *Pesachim* 72b: "All your words are . . . nought but mysteries."

23–24: Literally, "And at a hundred he is brother to the worm, repulsive to people, his raiment stained." Cf. Isaiah 14:19.

25–6: Cf. Job 16:4.

FEAR FIVE TO THE POWER OF FIVE (100)

Line 1: Literally, "Go in fear of five things from five."
6: Cf. Job 7:1 and Zechariah 9:8.

I QUARTERED THE TROOPS FOR THE NIGHT (131)

Cf. Latin poetry's *ubi sunt:* "Where now is your glory, Babylon, where is the terrible Nebuchadnezzar, and strong Darius and the famous Cyrus? Where now is Regulus, or where Romulus, or where Remus? . . ." Or Villon's "Where are the snows of yesteryear?" in his "Testament." Helen Weddell comments: "The [Latin] hymn of the great age, 1150 to 1250, has secret springs, and scholars have made a good, if non-proven case for Celtic and Arabic."

Line 5 and 7: Cf. Genesis 4:9: "Where is Abel your brother?"

9–10: Cf. *Shabbat* 114:a: "But R. Jannai said to his sons, 'My sons, bury me neither in white shrouds nor in black shrouds. White, lest I do not merit, and am like a bridegroom among mourners: black, in case I have merit, and am like a mourner among bridegrooms.'"

20: "These sleepers" in the original is "these crowds" or "these masses." I take it that the original refers both to HaNagid's own troops and to the "masters" who "slept on", but the ambiguity encourages an association (throughout the poem) with the other soldiers and peoples who once lived there and now "rest in the heart of the ground."

WHY REPEAT THE SINS (144)

Line 2: Cf. Psalms 78:40.
6: Cf. Genesis 8:3.

TIME DEFIES AND BETRAYS THE PATRICIANS (169)

Line 1: Cf. Deuteronomy 21:18
2: Literally, "haughty and proud." Cf. Numbers 32:13.
3: Literally, "lengthens the wandering of the separated."
4: Literally, "and it comes between twins as between north and south." None of my efforts to maintain the rhyme and content here were satisfactory, hence the departure from the original.

YOU FELT THE FEAR OF DEATH (179)

Line 1: Cf. Job 6:21.
2: Cf. Ezekiel 18:32.
3: Literally, "you bemoaned him." Cf. Psalms 69:21; Job 42:11: "And you bemoaned him. . ."
4: Cf. Lamentations 3:17.

WHY SHOULD THE HEARTS OF YOU PURISTS (195)

Lines 1–2: Cf. Proverbs 22:11: "He that loveth pureness of heart. . ."; Psalms 24:4; *Yebamot* 63:b: "Do not worry about tomorrow's trouble, for thou knowest not what the day may beget. Tomorrow may come and thou wilt be no more and so thou hast worried about a world which is not thine. . ."

3–4: Cf. *Berakhot* 9:b: "'I am that I am.' The Holy One, blessed be He, said to Moses: Go and say to Israel: I was with you in this servitude, and I shall be with you in the servitude of the [other] kingdoms. He said to Him: Lord of the Universe, sufficient is the evil in the time thereof!"

4: Cf. Proverbs 10:10; Isaiah 50:11: "And among the brands that ye have kindled this shall ye have of My hand: ye shall lie down in sorrow."

LUXURIES EASE (210)

Lines 1–2: Cf. Ecclesiastes 5:12: "There is a grievous evil which I have seen under the sun, namely, riches kept by the owner thereof to his hurt."

3: Cf. Isaiah 52:7; Song of Songs 1:10; 1 Kings 10:22: ". . . bringing gold, silver, ivory, apes and peacocks. So King Solomon exceeded all the kings of the earth in riches and in wisdom." Also Targum Onkelos for the verse.

4: Cf. Isaiah 17:13 and *Kalila and Dimna*, a fourth-century (CE) Indian cycle of fables which was available to HaNagid in an Arabic translation. The cycle was translated into Hebrew in the twelfth century. "For like it, was the male of the peacocks which, when it was pursued by a hunter, grew weary from the weight of its tail and was snared; and the weight of its tail was its misfortune and sorrow. Riches kept by its owner thereof to his hurt."

YOU'RE TRAPPED MY TONGUE (244)

Line 1: Cf. Jeremiah 33:1: "Moreover the Word of the Lord came unto Jeremiah the second time, while he was yet shut up in the court of the guard." Cf. Genesis 22:9: "And [Abraham] bound Isaac his son. . ."

3: Cf. Psalms 104:34.

5: Cf. 2 Samuel 18:17: "And they took Absolom, and cast him into the great pit. . . ."

7: Cf. Jeremiah 8:22: "Is there no balm in Gilead?"

8: Cf. Isaiah 14:11; Leviticus 2:6: "Thou shalt break it in pieces, . . . it is a meal offering."

FRIENDS, A FENCE SURROUNDS US (260)

This poem also appears in the "miscellaneous section" of *Ben Tehillim*.

Cf. "Earth to man," and many other poems by HaNagid, who often refers to the predestined place and time of his death, a medieval convention. Also see Bernard Lewis's translation of what most scholars consider the greatest religious poem in the Hebrew canon, *The Crown of Glory*, by HaNagid's protégé, Ibn Gabirol. See sections X–XXV, especially: "And Thou didst encompass the water with the sphere of air, the air that turns and turns and rests on its turnings," (X) and "Who can reckon Thy deeds of justice when Thou didst encompass the firmament of the moon with a second sphere, without break or breach..." (XIII). Also cf. *Niddah:* 31a: "His father supplies the semen of the white substance out of which are formed the child's bones, sinews, nails, the brain in his head and the white in his eye; his mother supplies the semen of the red substance out of which is formed his skin, flesh, hair, and the black of his eye."

3: Literally, "like the red and white in an egg."

4: Literally, "and the world is like an egg." Zemach suggests that the repetition of "egg" forces another meaning on the second appearance of the word, namely, "as nothing"—referring to the Talmudic use of the phrase "like an egg" or "like an olive" (e.g. *Berakhot* 45a) to mean something that it is negligible in size." "Shell" incorporates both this reading and Abramson's gloss: "like an egg, its shell encloses us."

5: Cf. 2 Samuel 22:2; Jeremiah 16:19.

7: Cf. Proverbs 8:22–23.

8–9: Cf. Isaiah 14:26: "This is the purpose that is purposed upon the whole earth; and this is the hand that is stretched out upon all the nations." Literally, "And what could we consider, when the plan is planned."

YOUTH BRINGS US (287)

Line 4: Literally, "negligence" or "transgression," for "decline".

HE WHO DEPENDS ON THE PRINCES (291)

ON THEIR COUCHES STRETCHED OUT AT THE TREASURY (296)

Cf. The Arabic of Dik al-Jinn al-Himsi (d. circa 850): "Time watches people in their sleep / A thief waiting for his chance" (trans. A. al-Udhari).

Line 1: Cf. Amos 6:4: "That lie upon beds of ivory, and stretch themselves upon their couches...."

2: Literally, "where someone will keep watch by the gate." Cf. Song of Songs 2:9.

4: Literally, "and time will come through your houses like a thief." Cf. Exodus 22:1: "If a thief be found breaking in..."

Line 1–2: Cf. Isaiah 34:14 and 13:21: "But wild-cats shall lie there; and their houses shall be full of ferrets; and ostriches shall dwell there, and satyrs shall dance there." Also Leviticus 17:7. The word for goats, *se'ir*, might also mean "satyr" here, as in Isaiah's vision of ruin.

3–4: Cf. 1 Samuel 25:22; 1 Kings 21:21; and *Baba Batra* 19:b: "Rabbah b. Bar Hana said: It is permissible for a man to make water on the side of another man's wall, as it is written, *And I will cut off from Ahab one that pisseth against the wall* . . . Even a creature whose way is to piss against a wall I will not leave him. And what is this? A dog."

<h2 style="text-align:center">SUFFER THE WORLD (306)</h2>

Line 1: The first word of the poem is hard to decipher, and the precise use of the word—*avod* (work)—is in this case unclear. Other readings suggest *amod* (set up or withstand) or *avor* (pass through). Yarden understands the first two lines as follows: "The worship of the world and soul together . . ."

3: Cf. Proverbs 1:4; Exodus 23:26. See also *Tshuvot Dunash*, line 1.

<h2 style="text-align:center">THE MARKET (314)</h2>

Several poems in the diwan begin like this one and employ the same form and locutions. The Hebrew end-rhyme (and often the internal rhyme at the hemistich) throughout the poem is on the syllable *dahm*, which by itself means blood.

Line 1: Cf. *Hullin* 9a: "Rab Judah stated in the name of Samuel, one may not eat of the slaughtering of any butcher who does not know the rules of *shechitah* (ritual slaughter)."

3–4: Literally, "and fatlings [or beasts] as many as fish of the sea, and much poultry, their day of great fear come." Cf. Ezekiel 47:10; Jeremiah 46:21: "Their day of calamity was come upon them."

5: Cf. Exodus 15:8: "The deeps were congealed in the heart of the sea. . ."

28: Cf. Ecclesiastes 12:13. Abramson notes "Ecclesiastes, with a slightly different thrust." Translations of the line in the biblical text vary from "This is the whole duty of man" to "This is the end of man" to "This is the whole person," and "For this applies to all mankind." "This" refers to "keeping the commandments," though HaNagid angles the verse at the preceding lines, which refer to human mortality. Abraham Ibn Ezra's commentary on Ecclesiastes (which post-dates HaNagid by nearly a century) resembles HaNagid's approach in this poem.

Ecclesiastes Rabbah XII:1 has: "'He [R. Levi] is as dear to Me as the whole world'; and when he died, people remarked, 'This is the whole man.'" The editors note: "He is equal to all men."

FLUTTER OR REST (333)

Line 1: Cf. Judges 7:3. The first word of the Hebrew, *tsphor*, has been translated in the ASV and JPS 1917 as "depart." NJPS has "flee like a bird."

SEE THE FRAUD FLOW BY (347)

Line 3: Cf. Proverbs 20:19: "He that goeth about as a talebearer revealeth secrets; therefore meddle not with him that openeth wide his lips."

Also, Job 31:27: "And my heart hath been secretly enticed"; Job 5:2; Hosea 7:11.

4: Literally, "like haters or foes."

THE EARTHQUAKE (350)

This poem also appears in *Ben Tehillim* (poem 110, Yarden), classified as a "nature poem." The superscription comes from there

Line 1–2: Cf. Psalms 23:1: "The Lord is my shepherd. . ." Psalms 139:3; Isaiah 18:4: "For thus hath the Lord said unto me: I will hold Me still, and I will look on in My dwelling place.'" Isaiah 62:1; Jeremiah 9:22; 1 Chronicles 29:1; Joshua 11:23.

3–4: Cf. Psalms 37:30: "The mouth of the righteous uttereth wisdom, and his tongue speaketh justice." Psalms 107:22, 145:5–6: "The glorious splendor of Thy majesty, and Thy wondrous works will I rehearse. And men shall speak of the might of Thy tremendous acts; and I will tell of Thy greatness"; Proverbs 12:18.

5–6: Cf. Psalms 104:5: "Who didst establish the earth upon its foundations, that it should not be moved. . ."

7–8: Cf. Malachi 3:11: "And I will rebuke the devourer for your good, and he shall not destroy the fruits of your land; neither shall your vine cast its fruit before the time in the field. . ."; Deuteronomy 8:8: "A land of . . . vines and

fig-trees. . ."; Habakkuk 3:17: "For though the fig-tree shall not blossom, neither shall fruit be in the vines; the labor of the olive shall fail, and the fields
shall yield no food"; Song of Songs 2:17.

10: Literally, "that each man's way is twisted" [morally]. Cf. Numbers 22:32.

11–12: Cf. Job 16:11: "God delivereth me to the ungodly, and casteth me into the
hands of the wicked."

13–14: Cf. Isaiah 34:4: "And all the host of heaven shall moulder away, and the
heavens shall be rolled together as a scroll; and all their host shall fall down,
as the leaf falleth off from the vine, and as a falling fig from the fig-tree."
Psalms 68:3; Leviticus 26:36: "And the sound of a driven leaf shall chase them;
and they shall flee as one fleeth from the sword, and they shall fall when none
pursueth"; Amos 6:5: "That thrum on the psaltery, that devise for themselves
instruments of music like David."

15–16: Cf. Amos 4:13; Jeremiah 43:12: "And he shall fold up the land of Egypt as
a shepherd foldeth up his garment."

17: Cf. Job 9:7: "Who commandeth the sun, and it riseth not. . ."

18: Cf. Deuteronomy 32:22: "For a fire . . . devoureth the earth with her pro-
duce, and setteth ablaze the foundations of the mountains." Psalms 104:32:
"He toucheth the mountains and they smoke."

20: Cf. Deuteronomy 8:7.

21–22: Cf. Psalms 29:6: "He maketh them also to skip like a calf; Lebanon and
Syrion like a young wild ox."

23: Cf. Ezekiel 16:57, 25:6, 28:24–25.

23–24: Cf. 2 Chronicles 24:13; Jeremiah 5:1; Isaiah 40:4: "Every valley shall be
lifted up, and every mountain and hill shall be made low; and the rugged shall
be made level, and the rough places a plain."

25–26: Cf. Ezekiel 3:12: "And I heard behind me the voice of a great rushing:
'Blessed be the glory of the Lord from His place'"; Habakkuk 3:16: "When I
heard, mine inward parts trembled. . ."; Psalms 119:158.

27–28: Cf. Psalms 99:1: "He is enthroned upon the cherubim: let the earth
quake."

29–30: Cf. Isaiah 2:19: "And men shall go into the caves of the rocks, and into
the holes of the earth, from before the terror of the Lord, and from the glory
of His majesty, when He ariseth to shake mightily the earth"; Proverbs 7:9:
"In the twilight, in the evening of the day, in the blackness of night and the
darkness."

31–32: Cf. 2 Kings 21:13: "I will wipe Jerusalem as a man wipeth a dish, wiping
it and turning it upside down"; *Baba Batra* 16a: "To turn the dish upside
down"; *Pesachim* 50a: "While R. Joshua b. Levi said: This refers to the peoples who are honored in this world, but will be lightly esteemed in the next
world. As was the case of R. Joseph the son of R. Joshua b. Levi, [who]
became ill and fell into a trance. When he recovered, his father asked him,

'What did you see?' 'I saw a topsy-turvy world,', he replied, 'the upper [class] underneath and the lower on top,' he replied. 'My son,' he observed, 'you saw a clear world.'"

33–34: Cf. Job 10:1: "My soul is weary of my life; I will give free course to my complaint, I will speak in the bitterness of my soul."

35–36: Cf. Isaiah 2:11: "The lofty looks of man shall be brought low, and the haughtiness of men shall be bowed down"; Isaiah 2:17.

37: Cf. Job 33:29: "Lo, all these things doth God work, twice, yea thrice, with a man."

38: Cf. Isaiah 24:19: "The earth is broken . . . the earth is crumbled in pieces, the earth trembleth and tottereth."

39–40: Cf. Hosea 7:1: "And the troop of robbers maketh a raid without."

41–42: Literally, "woman whose hair with length of days hadn't yet fallen out." Cf. Zechariah 8:4; Leviticus 13:40; *Ketubot* 108b-109a: "If a man promised a sum of money to his [prospective] son-in-law and then defaulted, let [his daughter] remain [single] until her hair turns white."

43–44: Cf. Job 26:11: "The pillars of heaven tremble, and are astonished at his rebuke"; Psalms 87:1.

45–46: Cf. *Bekhorot* 7:2: "And his knees do not knock against one another. . . ."

47–48: Cf. Job 9:6: "Who shaketh the earth out of her place, and the pillars thereof tremble"; Isaiah 40:21; Psalms 104:32: "Who looketh on the earth and it trembleth"; Isaiah 5:30.

49–52: Cf. Ezekiel 41:13; Psalms 11:3; Isaiah 19:10; Jeremiah 1:10; Deuteronomy 24:20.

53–55: Cf. 2 Chronicles 15:7; Genesis 32:12; Hosea 10:14; Jeremiah 47:3, 46:5; 1 Samuel 2:4.

56: Cf. Proverbs, 27:15, 31:10; Ruth 3:11; Isaiah 1:23.

57–59: Cf. Jeremiah 48:38; Amos 8:10; Leviticus 21:5. The image of the mother "scratching" or "cutting" her face—as the Hebrew has it— makes literal sense to anyone who has seen it in the Middle East, or on TV during the Gulf War of 1991. The Iraqi women were wailing and clawing at their faces with clenched hands in a downward motion. The eleventh-century Arabic poet Ibn al-Labband writes: "Young girls dropped their veils, clawed their faces, ripping their clothes" (trans. C. Franzen).

61: Cf. Isaiah 41:19.

62–64: Cf. 1 Samuel 21:10; Isaiah 46:2.

65: Cf. *Ketubot* 4:b; Isaiah 46:1–2.

66–67: Cf. Psalms 45:14; 2 Samuel 19:5.

68–69: Cf. Jeremiah 4:31; Isaiah 66:7.

70–71: Literally, "the soul of every man among his thoughts was like a ship sailing among waves." Cf. Job 17:11.

73: Cf. Leviticus 5:5.

74-75: Cf. Zephaniah 3:12; Isaiah 1:23; Psalms 10:18, 82:1-5: "God standeth in the congregation of God; In the midst of the judges He judgeth: How long will you judge unjustly, And respect the persons of the wicked? Judge the poor and fatherless; Do justice to the afflicted and destitute. . . . Deliver them out of the hand of the wicked. They know not, neither do they understand; They go about in darkness; All the foundations of the earth are moved."

77: Cf. Deuteronomy 32:15: "But Jeshurun waxed fat, and kicked—Thou didst wax fat, thou didst grow thick, thou dids't become gross."

79: Cf. Lamentations 4:18.

80: Cf. Isaiah 14:23.

81: The verse means that the destruction came from the western side of town.

82: Cf. Joel 2:7.

83: Cf. Jeremiah 9:14, 23:15; Genesis 25:29-30.

85-88: Cf. Job 22:16; 2 Samuel 14:7; Genesis 45:7.

89-90: Cf. Exodus 29:9; Ezekiel 26:16.

93: Cf. Isaiah 61:10.

95: Cf. Exodus 14:8.

98-99: I have added a line to the text, extending the biblical inlay from Job. Cf. Job 26:7.

100-102: Cf. Psalms 76:9: "Thou didst cause sentence to be heard from heaven: The earth feared, and was still."

103-104: Cf. Psalms 60:4: "Thou hast made the land to shake, Thou has cleft it; Heal the breaches thereof; for it tottereth"; Jeremiah 8:11; Isaiah 24:19.

TWO ECLIPSES (351)

These two eclipses took place precisely as described by HaNagid. The lunar eclipse occurred on November 8, 1044, between the hours of 11 PM and 2 AM; and the solar eclipse occurred on November 22, 1044, between 8 and 11 AM, reaching its height at 9 o'clock that morning. A second lunar eclipse took place on May 3, 1045, between 7 and 10 AM.

Line 2: Cf. Psalms 57:9; *Berakhot* 4:1; and *Sanhedrin* 16:b: "R. Isaac the son of R. Adda—others state, R. Isaac b. Abudimi—said: What verse [tells us of the harp hanging over David's bed]?—'Awake my glory, awake psaltery and harp; I will wake the dawn.'" *Berakhot* 10a: "He came out into the open air [of the world] and looked upon the stars and constellations and broke into song."

4: Cf. Jeremiah 13:23.

9: Cf. Leviticus 14:37 and Targum Onkelos. The word *sheka'arurah* is disputed. Leviticus reads "with hollow streaks, greenish and reddish." The Targum has *pehatin*, or "sunken spots" (as in leprosy). Ibn Janakh has "cracks, or fissures."

Sa'adia Gaon has "lines." Abramson suggests that HaNagid used the word to mean blackness or darkness, as does RaDaK. Yarden likewise reads "darkness."

11: Cf. Jeremiah 5:30 for *sha'arurah*. Abramson suggests that HaNagid meant "dirt" or "filth." Yarden suggests "darkness" or "dimness."

15: Cf. Job 16:16. The Targum here reads "defaced," "soiled," or "discolored." Abramson says "disfigured." Yarden reads "blackened." Job (JPS) has "reddened": "My face is reddened with weeping, and on my eyelids is the shadow of death."

16: Cf. Psalms 96:6.

19: Cf. Isaiah 40:22.

23: Cf. Song of Songs 6:10.

28: Cf. Isaiah 1:6.

30–31: Cf. Psalms 90:4.

38–39: Cf. Isaiah 63:5.

41: Cf. Leviticus 19:35.

43: Cf. Psalms 91:3; Proverbs 6:5.

45–46: Cf. Psalms 104:32; Isaiah 24:20.

47–48: Cf. Isaiah 50:9; Isaiah 51:8: "For the moth shall eat them up like a garment." Job 9:9. This strange image plays on the citations and the word *osh*—which means moth or worm on the one hand, and the Bear (the constellation) on the other. A similar image appears in a poem by Yehuda HaLevi (Brody, Vol. 1, p. 47): "They say that time has worn away at my love, but they might as well have said that a moth [*osh*] had eaten the Bear [*osh*]."

50: Cf. Psalms 91:4.

51–52: Cf. Jeremiah 25:30; Isaiah 63:3

53: Cf. 1 Chronicles 29:11.

54: Cf. 2 Samuel 8:4.

58–59: Cf. Zechariah 10:11; Jeremiah 4:31.

60–61: Cf. Proverbs 26:18; Psalms 91:5.

62–64: Cf. Daniel 12:2; Isaiah 26:19; Joel 3:4; Malachi 3:23.

65–66: Cf. Deuteronomy 29:24; Nehemiah 8:14; Joshua 22:5, 2 Chronicles 19:10, 7:19.

69–72: Cf. 1 Samuel 16:14; Judges 6:23; Isaiah 7:4. Fleischer notes: "While my spirit is far from you [because of my sins]."

THE TYRANT WHO RULES THE HOMELESS AND POOR (356)

Line 1: Cf. Isaiah 13:11, 29:20; Psalms 54:5; Job 6:23. For "rules with harshness" and "homeless and poor" cf. Leviticus 25:43; and Isaiah 58:7.

2: Cf. Isaiah 44:21; Lamentations 3:17; Deuteronomy 13:7.

4: Cf. Job 41:20; and Proverbs 7:23: "Till an arrow strike through his liver."
The prominent pun here involves the rhyme words of line 2 and 4. The last word of the poem is *kevaido* (his liver—in kabbalistic literature, the seat of power), which plays on the rhyme word of line 2—*kevodo* (his power/glory/honor). Corrupt with power, the leader forgets that he and his dispossessed subjects have a common fate. In the Hebrew the elevated long 'o' sound is brought down in the mouth by the "arrow" to a long 'a.'

MY SPIRIT (359)

Line 4: Literally, "Could you [suddenly] hate me and flee?"

THE BLACK OF MY HAIR (361)

Literally, "Time has bent my posture which had been like a *vuv* [the sixth letter of the Hebrew alphabet—which is upright in shape, much like an 'i' without the dot above it] into a bent *pei*, [the seventeenth letter, which is written somewhat like a backwards 'e'], and time has twisted my two legs like the leg of a *tuv* [the twenty-second letter of the alphabet, which looks like an upside-down u, with a foot attached to the end of it]." The metaphor of letters is fairly common in Arabic poetry (see "The Fawn"). Ibn Idris (twelfth century) writes: "The beauty spot on the page of her cheek punctuates the *nuns* [shaped a bit like a j] written there in the curls of her hair."

ASK THE DEAD AND THEY'LL TELL YOU (365)

2: Literally, "the secret of your creation. . ."
3–4: Cf. Psalms 35:10; Job 19:26.

SEND THE LORD TO THE PEOPLE (367)

The poem refers to the coming of the Messiah and the redemption of the Jews from exile, as the biblical inlay suggests.

Line 1–2: Cf. Malachi 3:1; Isaiah 49:9.
3–4: Literally, "they have brought them down to the shadow of death the dark ones." Abramson equates the "dark ones" or "dimness" with the "nations of the world."
5–6: Cf. Judges 5.28; Song of Songs 2:9; *Pesikta D'Rav Kahana HaHudash* 5:8: " 'Be-

hold, He standeth behind our wall' (Song of Songs 2:9), that is, by the western wall of the temple which will never be destroyed. 'He looketh in through the windows' (ibid)—that is, His presence is among us through the merit of the Patriarchs. 'He showeth himself through the lattice' (ibid)—that is, His presence is among us through the merit of the Matriarchs."

CAST YOUR BREAD (371)

Line 1: Cf. Ecclesiastes 11:1.
4: Literally, "and rob from you all that you did not cast [or send]."

KNOW OF THE LIMBS (365)

Line 1: Cf. Ezekiel 37:6. Lines 1–4 set up the weave of *Atsamot* (bones) *Ha'rkumot* (embroidered, decorated) and *Krumot* (covered)/*Atsumot* (powerful, great)— and *epher* (dust)/*aphar* (ash). I have tried to work this play into the English with the cross-weave of "Know" and "bone," "limbs" and "skin," "dust" and "reduced," "power" and "powder."

YOU MOCK ME NOW IN YOUR YOUTH (388)

Lines 3–4: Cf. *Pesikta de-Rab Kahana* 26:9: "Many a young ass has died and had its skin turned into saddlecloths for its dam's back." Also, *Sanhedrin* 52a: "Moses and Aaron once walked along, with Nadab and Abihu behind them, and all Israel following in the rear. Then Nadab said to Abihu, 'Oh that these old men might die, so that you and I should be the leaders of our generation.' But the Holy One, blessed be He, said unto them: 'We shall see who will bury whom.' R. Papa said: Thus men say: 'Many an old camel is laden with the hides of the young.'"

YOU THINK THERE'S NO HELL THAT WILL HOLD YOU (389)

Line 1: Cf. Job 14:13.
2: Cf. Job 11:12; *Baba Batra* 78:b: "This [*ayyar sihon*—the Gemara is explicating a mishna in which the word *sihon* (foal) appears] refers to one who follows his evil inclinations like a young ass [foal] who follows gentle talk [or a filly; i.e., that follows its desire—Rashi]."
4: Literally, "the end of the dew from the clouds and the waters of earth is a cistern." Cf. Jeremiah 6:7.

Cf. *The Ruba'iyat* #102: "You have seen the world and all you saw was nothing, / All you have said and heard, that too was nothing: / Running from Pole to Pole, there was nothing, / and when you looked at home, there was also nothing" (trans. P. Avery and J. Heath-Stubbs).

YOU LOOK THROUGH OPEN EYES (406)

Line 4: Literally, "and sin is caught in [tied to] your heart."

EVERYTHING HIDDEN (403)

Lines 5–6: Literally, "And yet when it's renewed you are glad with the gladness of your children in the way [immutable law] of the world."

❦ BIBLIOGRAPHY ❧

TEXTS OF THE POEMS IN HEBREW

Abramson, S., ed. Rabbi Shmuel HaNagid: *Ben Kohelet* [After Ecclesiastes]. Tel Aviv: Mahbarot LeSiphrut, 1952/3.

————. *Rabbi Shmuel HaNagid: Ben Mishle* [After Proverbs]. Tel Aviv: Mahbarot LeSiphrut, 1947/8.

Habermann, A. M., ed. *Rabbi Shmuel HaNagid: Shirei Milhamah* [R. Shmuel Ha-Nagid: Battle Poems]. Tel Aviv: Mahbarot LeSiphrut, 1963.

————. *Rabbi Shmuel HaNagid: Divan, Ve'Kolel Bo Sepher Ben Tehillim* [R. Shmuel HaNagid: The Diwan, Including After Psalms]. Tel Aviv: Mahbarot LeSiphrut, 1946/7.

Sassoon, D., ed. *Diwan Shmuel HaNagid: Published in the First Complete Edition.* Oxford: Oxford University Press, 1934.

Schirmann, J., ed. *HaShirah HaIvrit B'Sepharad U'Provence* [Hebrew Poems from Spain and Provence]. 2d Edition. Jerusalem and Tel Aviv: Mossad Bialik and Dvir Co., 1954, 1959.

Yarden, Dov, ed. *Divan Shmuel HaNagid* [The Collected Poetry of Samuel the Prince, 993–1056]: *Ben Tehillim* [The Son of Psalms]. 2d Edition. Jerusalem: Dov Yarden, 1985.

————. *Divan Shmuel HaNagid, Volume 2, Ben Mishle* [The Son of Proverbs]. Jerusalem: Dov Yarden, 1982.

————. *Divan Shmuel HaNagid, Volume 3, Ben Qoheleth* [The Son of Ecclesiastes]. 1st Edition. Jerusalem: Dov Yarden, 1992.

SOURCES FOR TRANSLATIONS IN ENGLISH

Abrahams, Israel, *Hebrew Ethical Wills*. Philadelphia: The Jewish Publication Society of America, 1926, 1954.

Carmi, T, ed. and trans. *The Penguin Book of Hebrew Verse*. New York: Viking, 1981.

Goldstein, David, ed. and trans. *The Jewish Poets of Spain, 900–1250*. Harmondsworth: Penguin, 1971.

Halkin, Hillel, trans. "Elegy for his Brother Isaac." *Ariel*, 79, 1990.

————. "The First Post Ancient Jew." *Commentary* (September 1993).

Scheindlin, Raymond P., ed. and trans. *Wine, Women, & Death: Medieval Hebrew Poems on the Good Life*. Philadelphia: The Jewish Publication Society, 1986.

Weinberger, Leon J., ed. and trans. *Jewish Prince in Moslem Spain: Selected Poems of Samuel Ibn Nagrela*. University: University of Alabama Press, 1973.

OTHER SOURCES

Biblical

The Holy Bible, Authorized King James Version. Oxford: Oxford University Press.
The Holy Scriptures, According to the Masoretic Text. Philadelphia: The Jewish Publication Society, 1917/1955.
The Book of Job. Trans. Stephen Mitchell. Berkeley: North Point Press, 1987.
The Jerusalem Bible. Jeruslem: Koren Publishers, 1980.
Tanakh, the Holy Scriptures: The New JPS Translation. Philadelphia: The Jewish Publication Society, 1985.

Post-biblical (listed in English translation when possible)

The Babylonian Talmud. Ed. I. Epstein. London: Soncino Press, 1990.
Bet Ha-Midrash. Ed. A. Jellinek. Jerusalem: Wahrmann Books, 1967.
Mekilta de-Rabbi Ishmael. Trans. Jacob Lauterbach. Philadelphia: Jewish Publication Society, 1933, 1961.
Midrash Rabbah. Ed. A. Myrkin. Yavneh, 1986.
Midrash Rabbah: Ruth and Ecclesiastes. Trans. Rabbi Dr. H. Freedman and Maurice Simon. London: Soncino Press, 1935.
Mikraot Gedolot, Jerusalem: Pa'er Offset Edition, 1972.
The Mishnah, A New Translation. Trans. Jacob Neusner. New Haven: Yale University Press, 1988.
Pesikta De-Rab Kahana. Trans. William G. Braude and Israel J. Kapstein. Philadelphia: The Jewish Publication Society, 1975.
Pesikta Rabbati. Trans. William G. Braude. New Haven: Yale University Press, 1968.
Pirke Aboth: The Ethics of the Talmud: Sayings of the Fathers. Trans. R. Travers Herford. New York: Schocken Books, 1945/1962.
Sepher HaAggadah. Ed. H. N. Bialik and Y. H. Ravnitzky. Tel Aviv: Dvir, 1960/1987.

ADDITIONAL BIBLIOGRAPHY
(books cited and background reading)

Ali, Ahmed, trans. *Al-Qur'an.* Princeton: Princeton University Press, 1988.
Al-Udhari, Abdullah, trans. *Fireflies in the Dark: Classical Arabic Poetry.* Menard: London, 1974.
Arberry, A. J. *Aspects of Islamic Civilization.* New York: A. S. Barnes & Co., 1964.
————, trans. *The Koran.* Oxford: Oxford University Press, 1964.
Aristotle. *Complete Works of Aristotle.* Revised Oxford trans., ed. Jonathan Barnes. Princeton: Princeton University Press, 1984.

————. *Aristotle's Theory of Poetry and Fine Art, With a Critical Text and Translation of The Poetics.* Trans. S. H. Butcher. New York: Dover, 1951.

Ashtor, Eliyahu. *The Jews of Moslem Spain.* 3 vols. Philadelphia: Jewish Publication Society, 1973.

————. "The Number of Jews in Muslim Spain" [Hebrew]. *Zion* 28 (1963).

Avery, Peter, and John Heath-Stubbs. *The Ruba'iyat of Omar Khayyam.* London: Penguin, 1989.

Bargebuhr, F. P. *The Alhambra: A Cycle of Studies on the Eleventh Century in Moorish Spain.* Berlin: Walter de Gruyter & Co., 1968.

Baron, N. "Toward the Study of the Sources of *Ben Mishlei* of R. Samuel Ha-Nagid" [Hebrew]. In *Proceedings of the World Congress of Jewish Studies* 1. Jerusalem: 1947.

Baron, Salo Wittmayer. *A Social and Religious History of the Jews* Vols. 3–8. New York: Columbia University Press, 1958.

Beinart, H. *Atlas of Medieval Jewish History.* New York: Simon and Schuster, 1992.

Ben Elazar, Ya'akov, trans. (Hebrew). *Kalila Wa'Dimna.* Ed., J. Derenbourg. Paris: F. Vieweg, Libraire-Editeur, 1881.

Bialik, Hayyim N. *Kol Kitvei H. N. Bialik* [The Complete Works of H. N. Bialik]. Tel Aviv: Dvir, 1937–38 / 1964–65.

Brann, Ross. *The Compunctious Poet: Cultural Ambiguity and Hebrew Poetry in Muslim Spain.* Baltimore: Johns Hopkins University Press, 1991.

Coomaraswamy, A. K. *Traditional Art and Symbolism.* Princeton: Princeton University Press, 1977.

Dodds, Jerrilynn D. *Al-Andalus: The Art of Islamic Spain.* New York: The Metropolitan Museum, 1992.

Dozy, Reinhart. *Spanish Islam: A History of the Moslems in Spain.* Trans. Francis Griffin Stokes. London: Frank Cass, 1972.

Dunash ben Labrat. *Tshuvot Dunash.* London and Edingburgh: Hevrat Me'orrei Yeshanim, 1855. Reprinted in *Arba'a Sepharim Niphtachim,* Jerusalem: Wagshal, no date.

Encyclopedia of Islam. See articles on Al-Andalus, Kasida, Judeo-Arabic literature. Leiden: Brill 1978–79.

Encyclopedia Judaica. See articles on Hebrew poetry, Spain, Samuel HaNagid, Hebrew Grammar, Hebrew language, Hebrew prosody, Hebrew poetry, and others. Jerusalem: Keter, 1972.

Fitzgerald, Edward, trans. *The Rubaiyat of Omar Khayyam the Astronomer-Poet of Persia.* New York: Books, Inc., n.d.

Fleischer, Ezra. *Shirat Hakodesh Ha'Ivrit Be'Yamei Benayyim* [Liturgical Poetry in the Middle Ages]. Jerusalem: Keter, 1975.

Franzen, Cola, *Poems of Andalusia.* San Francisco: City Lights, 1969, 1985.

Glatzer, Nahum, ed. *The Passover Haggadah.* New York: Shocken Books, 1953, 1981.

Goitein, S. D. *Jews and Arabs: Their Contacts through the Ages*. New York: Schocken Books, 1955.

———. "Jewish Trade in the Mediterranean at the Beginning of the Eleventh Century", [Hebrew]. *Tarbiz* 36:4 (1967).

———. *Letters of Medieval Jewish Traders Translated from the Arabic*. Princeton: Princeton University Press, 1973.

———. *Mediterranean Society*. Vols. 1–5. Berkeley: University of California Press, 1967–88.

———. "The Title and Office of the Nagid, A Re-examination." *JQR* 53 (1962–63).

Gombrich, E. H. *The Sense of Order: A Study of the Psychology of Decorative Art*. Ithaca: Cornell University Press, 1979.

Grabar, Oleg. *The Formation of Islamic Art*. New Haven: Yale University Press, 1973, 1987.

———. *The Mediation of Ornament*. Princeton: Princeton University Press, 1992.

HaLevi, Yehuda. *The Diwan* [Hebrew]. Ed. Haim Brody. Berlin: Mekitze Nirdamim, 1894–1930 (repr. with introduction, bibliography, additions, and indices by A. M. Habermann, Farnsborough: Gregg International, 1971).

Ibn Daud, Abraham. *Sefer ha-Qabbalah: The Book of Tradition*. Ed. and trans. G. D. Cohen. Philadelphia: The Jewish Publication Society, 1967.

Ibn Ezra, Moshe b. Ya'akov. *Kitab al-Muhadara wal-Mudhakara (Sepher HaIyyunim veHaDiyyunim: Poetica Hebraica)*. Hebrew trans. A. S. Halkin. Jerusalem: Mekitze Nirdamim, 1975.

Ibn Gabirol, Shlomo. *Shirei Hol* [Secular Poems]. Ed. Haim Brody and Haim Schirmann. Jerusalem: The Schocken Institute for Jewish Research 1974.

———. *The Kingly Crown*. Trans. B. Lewis. London: Valentine Mitchell, 1961.

Ibn Janakh, R. Yonah. *Sepher HaShorashim* [The Book of Roots]. Berlin: Mekitze Nirdamim, 1896.

Ibn Khaldun, Abd ar-Rahman. *The Muqaddimah: An Introduction to History*. Trans. Franz Rosenthal. Princeton: Princeton University Press, 1967.

Kimchi, R. David (RaDak). *Sepher HaShorashim* [The Book of Roots]. Berlin: Impensis G. Bethge, 1847 / Jerusalem, 1967, ed. N. J. Dawood.

Kozody, Neil. "Reading Medieval Hebrew Love Poetry." *AJS Review* 2 (1977).

Kugel, James. "On All of Hebrew Poetry." *Prooftexts* 2:2 (1982): 209–21.

Levin, Y. *The Embroidered Coat: The Genres of Hebrew Secular Poetry in Spain* [Hebrew]. Tel Aviv: Tel Aviv University Press, 1980.

———. "On Plagiarism and Originality in the Hebrew Poetry in Spain in the Middle Ages." *Peles*. Tel Aviv, (1980).

———. "The Battle Poems of Samuel HaNagid, against the Background of Classical Arabic Heroic Poetry" [Hebrew]. In *HaSiphrut*. Vol. 1.

———. *Shmuel Hannagid: [His Life and His Poems]*. Tel Aviv: Hakibbutz Hame'uchad, 1962–63.

———. "Toward the Study of *Ben Mishlei* of R. Samuel HaNagid" [Hebrew]. *Tarbiz* 29:2 (1960).

————. "Weeping Over Ruins and the Wandering Night-Vision" [Hebrew]. *Tarbiz* 36:3 (1967).

Mardus, J. C., and Powys Mathers. *The Book of The Thousand Nights and One Night*. Vols. 1–4. London: The Folio Society, 1958.

Margulioth, Mordechai. *Hilkhot Hannagid* [A Collection of the Extant Halakhic Writings of R. Shmuel Hannagid]. Jerusalem: American Academy for Jewish Research, 1962.

Middleton, Christopher, and Leticia Garza-Falcon. *Andalusian Poems*. Boston: Godine, 1992.

Monroe, James T. *Hispano-Arabic Poetry: A Student Anthology*. Berkeley: University of California Press, 1974.

Nicholson, R. A. *A Literary History of the Arabs*. Cambridge: Cambridge University Press, 1930.

Nykl, A. R. *Hispano-Arabic Poetry and its Relation with Old Provençal Troubadors*. Baltimore: J. H. Furst, 1946.

Pagis, Dan. *Hebrew Poetry of the Middle Ages and the Renaissance*. Berkeley: University of California Press, 1991.

————. *HaShir Debur al Ophnav* [Poetry Aptly Explained: Studies and Essays on Medieval Hebrew Poetry]. Ed. Ezra Fleischer. Jerusalem: Magnes Press, 1993.

————. *Shirat HaChol VeTorat HaShir LeMoshe Eben Ezra U'Vene Doro* [The Secular Poetry and Poetic Theory of Moshe Ibn Ezra]. Jerusalem: Mossad Bialik, 1970.

————. *Hidush U'Masoret B'Shirat HaChol HaIvrit: Sepharad Ve'Italia* [Change and Tradition in Secular Hebrew Poetry: Spain and Italy]. Jerusalem: Keter, 1976.

Ratzhaby, Yehudah. "On the Sources of Ben Mishlei and Ben Kohelet" [Hebrew]. *Tarbiz* 3 (1956).

————. "Night-Visions in the Poetry of HaNagid and Ibn Gabirol" [Hebrew]. *Tarbiz* 47 (1977–78).

————. "The Wine Poetry of R. Samuel the Nagid" [Hebrew]. *Bar Ilan University Annual* 9:1 (1972).

————. "Love in the Poetry of Shmuel HaNagid" [Hebrew]. *Tarbiz* 39 (1970–71).

————. "Arabic Proverbs in Medieval Literature" [Hebrew]. *Otsar Yehudei Sepharad* 4 (1961).

————. "The Language of R. Shmuel HaNagid's *Ben Mishle*" [Hebrew]. *Bar Ilan Annual* 4–5 (1957/58).

————. "On the Sources of HaNagid's Proverbs" [Hebrew]. *Otsar Yehudei Sepharad* 3 (1960).

Rosen-Moked, Tova. "A Hebrew Mariner and the Sea Monster." *Mediterranean Historical Review* 1:2 (1986).

Roth, Norman. "Deal Gently with the Young Man: Love of Boys in Medieval Hebrew Poetry of Spain." *Speculum* 57 (1982): 20–51.

————. "The Jews and the Muslim Conquest of Spain." *Jewish Social Studies* 38 (1976).

————. "Jewish Reaction to the Arabiyya and the Renaissance of Hebrew in Spain." *Journal of Semitic Studies* 28:1 (1983).

Sa'adia Gaon. *The Book of Beliefs and Opinions*. Trans. from the Arabic and the Hebrew by Samuel Rosenblatt. New Haven: Yale University Press, 1948, 1976.

Sassoon, D. S. "Diwan of the Vizier Samuel Hannaghid." *Jewish Chronicle Supplement*, March 28, 1924.

Scheindlin, Raymond. "Moshe Ibn Ezra on the Legitimacy of Poetry." *Medievalia et Humanistica*, N.S. 7 (1976).

Schirmann, J. *Shirim Hadashim min HaGenizah* [New Hebrew Poems from the Genizah]. Jerusalem: Publications of the Israel Academy of Sciences and Humanities, 1965.

————. *LeToldot HaShira Ve'HaDrama Ha'Ivrit: I* [Studies in the History of Hebrew Poetry and Drama: Vol. 1]. Jerusalem: Mossad Bialik, 1979.

————. "The Ephebe in Medieval Hebrew Poetry." *Sefarad* 15 (1955): 55–68.

————. "The Function of the Hebrew Poet in Medieval Spain." *Jewish Social Studies* 16 (1954): 235–52.

————. "How Should We Recite the Metrical Poetry of Our Spanish Poets?" [Hebrew], *Proceedings of the World Congress of Jewish Studies* I. Jerusalem: 1947.

————. "Samuel Hannagid, the Man, the Soldier, the Politician." *Jewish Social Studies* 13 (1951).

Sells, Michael A. *Desert Tracings: Six Classical Arabian Odes*. Middletown: Wesleyan University Press, 1989.

Septimus, B. "On Rabbinic Response to the Poetry of Spain" [Hebrew]. *Tarbiz* 53 (1984).

Stetkevych, Jaroslav. *The Zephrys of Najd*. Chicago: University of Chicago Press, 1993.

————. "Confluence of Arabic and Hebrew Literature." *Journal of Near Eastern Studies* 32 1/2 (1973).

Stillman, Norman A. *The Jews of Arab Lands: A History and Source Book*. Philadelphia: Jewish Publication Society, 1979.

————. "Aspects of Jewish Life in Islamic Spain." In *Aspects of Jewish Culture in the Middle Ages*. Ed. Paul E. Szarmach. Albany: SUNY Press, 1979.

Theognis. *Hesiod and Theognis*. Trans. Dorothea Wender. Harmondsworth/London: Penguin, 1973.

Tsemach, Adi, and Tovah Rosen-Moked. *Yetsirah MeHukamah: Iyyun b'Shirei Shmuel HaNagid* [A Sophisticated Work: Studies in the Poetry of Shmuel HaNagid]. Jerusalem: Keter, 1983.

Tsur, Reuven. *How Do the Sound Patterns Know They Are Expressive? The Poetic Mode of Speech Perception*. Tel Aviv: Israel Science Publishers, 1987.

————. *Medieval Hebrew Poetry in a Double Perspective: The Versatile Reader and Hebrew Poetry in Spain* [Hebrew]. Tel Aviv: University Publishing Projects, 1987.

von Grunebaum, Gustave E., ed. "The Concept of Plagiarism in Arabic Theory." *Journal of Near Eastern Studies* 3 (1944).

Waddell, H. *Medieval Latin Lyrics*. Harmondsowrth: Penguin Books, 1929, 1952.

Walzer, Richard. "Arabic Transmission of Greek Thought to Medieval Europe." *Bulletin of the John Rylands Library*, Vol. 29. (1945)

Wasserstein, David. *The Rise and Fall of the Party Kings*. Princeton: Princeton University Press, 1985.

Weiss, J. "Court Culture and Court Poetry" [Hebrew]. *Proceedings of the World Congress of Jewish Studies* 1 (1952).

Wightman, G.B.H, and Abdullah Al-Udhari, trans. *Birds Through a Ceiling of Alabaster*. London: Penguin, 1975.

Wolfson, Harry. *Three Jewish Philosophers: Philo, Saadya Gaon, Jehuda Halevi*. New York: Atheneum, 1958.

Wood, Ramsey. *Kalil and Dimna*. New York: Knopf, 1980.

Yellin, David. *Torat HaShirah HaSepharadit* [The Poetics of the Spanish-Hebrew Poets]. Jerusalem: Magnes Press and the Hebrew University, 1940, 1978.

————. *Ketavim Nivharim [Selected Writings]*. Vol. 2, Jerusalem: Kiryat Sepher, 1939.

Zinberg, Israel, ed. *A History of Jewish Literature, Vol. 1: The Arabic Spanish Period*. Trans. B. Martin. Hoboken: Ktav, 1972.

Yosef, Shaul Abdullah. *Givat Shaul*. Vienna: IG. Unger, 1923.

Zulay, Menahem. *The Liturgical Poetry of Sa'adya Gaon and His School* [Hebrew]. Jerusalem: The Schocken Institute for Jewish Research, 1964.

The Lockert Library of Poetry in Translation

George Seferis: Collected Poems (1924–1955), translated, edited, and introduced by Edmund Keeley and Philip Sherrard

Collected Poems of Lucio Piccolo, translated and edited by Brian Swann and Ruth Feldman

C. P. Cavafy: Collected Poems, translated by Edmund Keeley and Philip Sherrard and edited by George Savidis

Benny Andersen: Selected Poems, translated by Alexander Taylor

Selected Poetry of Andrea Zanzotto, edited and translated by Ruth Feldman and Brian Swann

Poems of René Char, translated and annotated by Mary Ann Caws and Jonathan Griffin

Selected Poems of Tudor Arghezi, translated by Michael Impey and Brian Swann

"The Survivor" and Other Poems by Tadeusz Różewicz, translated and introduced by Magnus J. Krynski and Robert A Maguire

"Harsh World" and Other Poems by Ángel González, translated by Donald D. Walsh

Ritsos in Parentheses, translations and introduction by Edmund Keeley

Salamander: Selected Poems of Robert Marteau, translated by Anne Winters

Angelos Sikelianos: Selected Poems, translated and introduced by Edmund Keeley and Philip Sherrard

Dante's "Rime," translated by Patrick S. Diehl

Selected Later Poems of Marie Luise Kaschnitz, translated by Lisel Mueller

Osip Mandelstam's "Stone," translated and introduced by Robert Tracy

The Dawn Is Always New: Selected Poetry of Rocco Scotellaro, translated by Ruth Feldman and Brian Swann

Sounds, Feelings, Thoughts: Seventy Poems by Wisława Szymborska, translated and introduced by Magnus J. Krynski and Robert A. Maguire

The Man I Pretend to Be: "The Colloquies" and Selected Poems of Guido Gozzano, translated and edited by Michael Palma, with an introductory essay by Eugenio Montale

D'Après Tout: Poems by Jean Follain, translated by Heather McHugh

---